EXPLORING
THE NENE WAY

Countryside Books' walking guides cover most areas of England and Wales and include the following series:

County Rambles
Walks for Motorists
Exploring Long Distance Paths
Literary Walks
Pub Walks

A complete list is available from the publishers.

EXPLORING
THE NENE WAY

Mia Butler

COUNTRYSIDE BOOKS
NEWBURY, BERKSHIRE

First published 1992
© Mia Butler 1992

COUNTRYSIDE BOOKS
3 Catherine Road
Newbury, Berkshire

ISBN 1 85306 176 X

Cover photograph by courtesy of
British Waterways

Typeset by Acorn Bookwork, Salisbury, Wiltshire
Produced through MRM Associates Ltd., Reading
Printed by JW Arrowsmith Ltd., Bristol

To JC, for whom
the long trek began

Contents

Introduction   11

Walk 1   Badby, The Everdons, Preston Capes and Fawsley
Park   17
(Nene Way – Badby to Little Everdon)

Walk 2   Newnham and Upper Weedon   23
(Nene Way – Little Everdon to Upper Weedon)

Walk 3   Nether Heyford and the Grand Union Canal   29
(Nene Way – Weedon to Nether Heyford)

Walk 4   Kislingbury   37
(Nene Way – Nether Heyford to Upton)

Walk 5   Northampton   43
(Nene Way – Upton to Northampton)

Walk 6   Washlands Reservoir and Clifford Hill   51
(Nene Way – Northampton to Clifford Hill)

Walk 7   Cogenhoe and Whiston   59
(Nene Way – Clifford Hill to Whiston Lock)

Walk 8   Irchester Country Park and Wellingborough   65
(Nene Way – Whiston Lock to Black Bridge)

Walk 9   Higham Ferrers and Irthlingborough   75
(Nene Way – Black Bridge to Irthlingborough)

Walk 10   Woodford, Denford and Ringstead   81
(Nene Way – Irthlingborough to Denford)

Walk 11   Titchmarsh Nature Reserve and Thrapston Lake   87
(Nene Way – Denford to Aldwincle)

Walk 12   Wadenhoe, The Linches and Lyveden New Bield   93
           (Nene Way – Aldwincle to The Linches)

Walk 13   Barnwell, Ashton and Polebrook   101
           (Nene Way – The Linches to Ashton)

Walk 14   Oundle, Cotterstock and Ashton   107

Walk 15   Fotheringhay and Woodnewton   113
           (Nene Way – Ashton to Fotheringhay)

Walk 16   Nassington, Wansford and Old Sulehay Forest   121
           (Nene Way – Fotheringhay to Wansford)

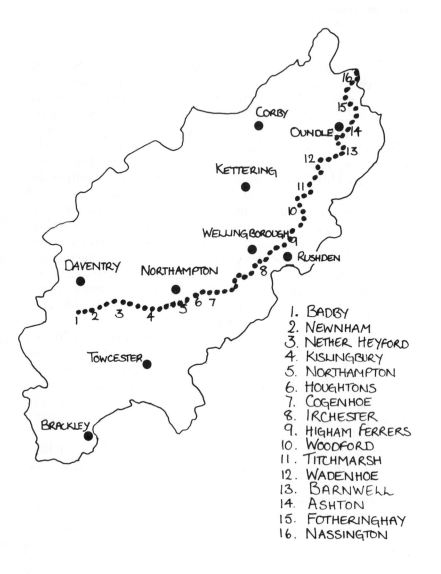

1. BADBY
2. NEWNHAM
3. NETHER HEYFORD
4. KISLINGBURY
5. NORTHAMPTON
6. HOUGHTONS
7. COGENHOE
8. IRCHESTER
9. HIGHAM FERRERS
10. WOODFORD
11. TITCHMARSH
12. WADENHOE
13. BARNWELL
14. ASHTON
15. FOTHERINGHAY
16. NASSINGTON

10

Introduction

Throughout the centuries, the Nene Valley has been the venue of successive settlements. Artefacts from Roman times, and the legacy of the many names incorporating 'chester', indicate the significance of the broad valley. In modern times, the river Nene is strictly controlled, and no longer subject to the vagaries of severe flooding, which used to cause frequent havoc. The meandering river, which rises close to the historic beacon site of Arbury Hill (734 ft) not far from Badby in the south of the county, was an important trade highway, and a very valid reason for the ensuing habitation. Now, extensive sand and gravel extraction may mar the scenery in places, but workings have exposed a fabulous mosaic floor of Roman origin, found at a shallow depth below ground level. Many archaeological treasures have been unearthed in similar circumstances, and such intrusions, when effectively and ultimately restored, will again provide haven and habitat for the dwindling wildlife.

Coal and grain were hauled up from the Fen by 'lighters', and on return, cargoes of locally quarried stone were loaded for distribution. Many mills for cereal, and paper, lined the water's edge, and some of these buildings now tastefully renovated remain today, serving as a reminder of such vital industries. Some even retain the old wharves, and Bugbrooke Mill, near to Northampton, stands on a site known to have accommodated a mill since AD 300.

The bordering, and then prolific, rushes were utilised in later times for the traditional village crafts of basket and mat making, thatching, and the stuffing of horse collars. Grazing animals on rich pastures provided food, and leather and wool for clothing. The thick woodlands were a source of building materials, stakes for fencing and thatching, cattle pens, carts and wheels, a refuge for deer, and had a thousand other uses. A

11

colourful patchwork of flora covered the slopes, where herbs might be found for medicines, and there were productive, lush water-meadows, long before the hideous roads and motorways encroached to carve up the landscape, devastating some of these most precious areas.

Man built fortified manors and castles, hence the numerous motte and bailey sites, great medieval houses, monuments and memorials, and glorious places of worship, such as the revered, more than 1,000 year old All Saints parish church which dominates Earls Barton. A theory exists that this was once the site of an Iron Age hill fort. A dazzling array of architectural styles are on offer in archaic colleges and other seats of learning, reflecting the wealth of earlier ages, alongside the more humble abodes like cottages and almshouses. Elegant dwellings built of the local ironstore and limestone, often featured in contrasting bands, can be seen in the plethora of charming villages and outlying farmsteads.

Evident too, as the river winds along, are the old towpaths of river and canal, with packbridges worn smooth by the feet of man and animals, moving slowly across the valley floor from one community to another. There are also sleepy hamlets where little has changed but the residents! Stone bridges, from Gothic style to stark modern concrete, and high, arched con-structions of wood to allow for the passage of boats, span the river, as well as shallow fords flowing beneath solid ancient cutwaters. Banks of graceful foliage have survived here and there, where the walker should keep an alert eye open for a flash of the brilliant kingfisher, or the haughty heron, standing aloof on one leg!

The Nene Way was originally proposed by Northampton-shire County Council and was developed over a five year period with financial aid from Northamptonshire County Council and the Countryside Commission. The early part of the task was carried out by fieldworkers employed on the Community Programme, and later, by the Employment Training Division. Comprehensive information and interpretation was supplied by Countryside Access and the Heritage Project teams employed by the County Council. It was opened by HRH the Duke of Gloucester, at Barnwell, near Oundle, in April 1990.

This 70 mile walk is a linking progression of Rights of Way, bridleways and byways, negotiated footpaths etc, and is identified by a succession of oak stiles and 'Nene Way' fingerposts. Landowners were consulted prior to the necessary work of replacing worn furnishings, and the installation of bridges. Various approaches to the route were redesigned and improved, and steps constructed to facilitate easier access. Leaflets of the entire route of the Nene Way are produced separately or as a set, along with other Countryside Walks, from Northamptonshire Countryside Services.

The Nene Way is very much an 'up hill and down dale' path, keeping company with the river but departing now and again to whisk the traveller up the rise and back down again, crossing locks, and even going through built up areas, such as the stretch through the historic county town of Northampton.

The whole of the Nene Way is incorporated into this book and if you are doing the full 70 mile walk the relevant sections are clearly indicated in each chapter. For those who prefer to sample the delights of the Nene Valley in smaller doses, anything from 2½ to 8 miles, I have arranged the book as a series of circular walks, taking in sections of the Nene Way and the surrounding glorious countryside. Each of these rambles will give you a morning or afternoon's enjoyment in the open air.

Sketch maps are supplied for each walk but the relevant Ordnance Survey map in the 1 : 50 000 series is noted should you wish to follow the route in more detail. Each walk includes a section of historical notes to points of interest along the way.

The Nene Way ends at Wansford, on the border with Cambridgeshire, a comely village laced with history, set around a

13

handsome, many arched stone bridge. However, in passing beneath the bridge carrying the busy A1, the long distance path continues toward Peterborough and the spacious Ferry Meadows Country Park, and ultimately to The Wash, on the east coast.

Mia Butler
Spring 1992

ACKNOWLEDGEMENTS

Jean Draper for the artwork
Jean Jolley & Pat Rolph
Marian Pipe
Anne & Frank Groome
Sue Payne
Friends & colleagues in Northamptonshire County Council &
especially those in Countryside Services
The Forestry Commission
Northamptonshire Federation of Women's Institutes

Problems arising along the Nene Way should be reported to the appropriate Officers as below:

Principal Rights of Way Officer
Area 1 Office
73 London Road
Kettering
Northants
Tel: Kettering 524100.

Principal Rights of Way Officer
Area 2 Office
Arnex House
London Road
Daventry
Northants
Tel: Daventry 301001.

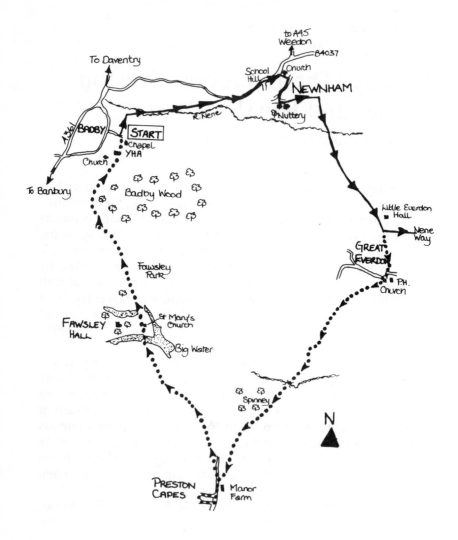

Badby, The Everdons, Preston Capes and Fawsley Park

(Nene Way – Badby to Little Everdon)

Introduction: The Nene Way begins in the attractive village of Badby. Here it links with another County Walk, the Knightley Way (10.5 miles), which in turn, at Greens Norton, connects with the Grafton Way (12 miles) to Cosgrove, thus spanning the shire from the south west to the north east borders. The river Nene, from which the walk takes its name, rises close by in the lee of Arbury Hill, the county's highest point and well known for its earthworks, in close proximity to Daventry. This is an exceptionally seductive sector of the Way, lying at the extreme end of the Cotswolds and blessed with ample parks and woodlands.

This circular walk also begins in Badby, where the green is graced by magnificent chestnut trees, and follows the Nene Way along the lovely valley of the river Nene to Newnham and the Everdons. Some say that it was the peaceful churchyard of Great Everdon which provided the model for Gray's famous 'Elegy in a Country Churchyard'. Past Everdon Hill, the walk reaches the pretty village of Preston Capes. Manor Farm House here was built on the site of an 11th century castle. Then down the hill towards the glorious parkland of Fawsley Hall with its elegant fallow deer and noble house. Badby Wood, through which the walk returns to Badby, is renowned for the display of bluebells in the spring.

Distance: Approximately 8 miles, which includes some prot-
racted valley slopes. Nene Way section about 2.7 miles. OS
Landranger series 1:50 000 map 152 Northampton & Milton
Keynes.

Refreshments: In Badby, The Maltsters Arms and The Wind-
mill Inn Hotel, also The Romer Arms at Newnham. The
Plough at Everdon is adjacent to the church, and all three
villages have small shops. The youth hostel at Badby is situated
on Church Green, via Vicarage Hill from Main Street. It is self
catering, well equipped, and open after 5 pm daily. Phone
0327-703883 for the Warden.

How to get there: Badby is on the A361 Daventry to Banbury
road, or 4 miles due west of Weedon on the A45 from Northampton. There are regular weekday bus services on the former
route only. Considerate street parking for cars is requested.

Nene Way – Badby to Little Everdon: The Way starts at Badby
and follows the course of the circular walk until it reaches
Little Everdon. To continue on the Nene Way, turn to Walk
Two.

The Walk: From the green at Badby, turn left into Chapel
Lane and proceed to the last house, opposite the United
Reformed chapel. Here the first oak Nene Way post appears,
and it continues to be well signed throughout.

Initially, the path runs beside a trickling stream at the foot of
homes and gardens, ablaze with colour in summer, and then
crosses three low lying fields to meet the road on the edge of
Newnham.

On the green, a unique decorative circular iron seat wraps
around the hawthorn tree outside the general store and The
Romer Arms. Carry on up School Hill past the thatched
cottage and barn, war memorial and old well with its tiled roof.

At the church of St Michael and All Angels, turn into the gate and follow the Nene Way through the churchyard on the sunken path, between high banks and moss covered walls to another sealed well, where a peek over the parapet will reveal a surprise!

Go down the narrow leafy lane to the T-junction and turn left to The Nuttery, a commercial nut farm, growing a catch crop of snowdrops in the spring.

Follow the Nene Way posts, fixed at intervals and initially on a group of three willows and a telegraph pole, over several sloping fields to Little Everdon Hall, a private residence of great charm. Laid out in considerable parkland, the meticulous jumps for the acclaimed Everdon Horse Trials are a permanent fixture.

Skirting the Hall, head for the yard and exit by stone steps cunningly fashioned in the handsome wall. Opposite is The Old House, with mullioned windows, circa 1690, one of the few in this tiny hamlet. For the through route on the **Nene Way**, continue at Walk Two.

For the circular walk, take the road forward up the hill to Great Everdon bearing right toward the massive ironstone church of St Mary, built on a mound, where the fingerpost 'to Preston Capes' points to the path overhung by dark yews alongside the village hall. On the gate, 'God's Little Acre' is an apt description of the graveyard, considered by some to be the place featured in Thomas Gray's famous 'Elegy', as opposed to Stoke Poges. The poet was often to be seen about the village whilst visiting his uncle, the Reverend William Antrobus, who was the rector here from 1729–44.

Follow the succession of waymarks (though not every hedge-line is marked) along slanting pastures, with the plateau of Everdon Hill to the right (this could provide an alternative route to join the Knightley Way at Fawsley Park, and affords splendid views).

Preston Capes may be glimpsed on reaching Kingbrook

Spinney, guiding the walker to exit onto the road. It will be very rewarding to take a short village loop just up the hill, via Church Way and Old Forge Lane, to enjoy the delightful tableau of this enchanting little diversion. Manor Farm House was built on the site of an ancient castle, founded in the 11th century.

Retrace your steps now down the hill and look out for the elegant fallow deer in the park, with their smart black and white tails.

The path now joins the Knightley Way, indicated by large circular white discs. Passing areas of plantations, come to Fawsley Park and its fine lakes. Cross between The Canal and Big Water, in the valley of the river Cherwell, toward the church of St Mary. Do pause here in this serene environment to savour the vista of the estate and noble Fawsley Hall. Set with a spectacular oriel window, buttresses and bays, it dates from the 17th century.

Cross the lane on the bend and follow the Knightley Way to the up-and-over ladder stiles and rolling parkland studded with stately beeches, though sadly some have now fallen with the ravages of time. Walk on to Badby Wood, noted for the stunning display of bluebells in season.

On leaving the woodland and traversing two more fields, Badby village lies comfortably nestled in the dells ahead.

Historical Notes

Badby: First chronicled in AD 833, Badby was then in the charge of the abbey of Croyland, granted at that time by King Witlaf of Mercia. It passed to the abbey of Evesham, before being returned to the former abbot at the time of the Domesday survey. In 1246, at the instigation of the abbot, Badby Wood was enclosed as parkland, by permission of the Crown.

In 1542, after the Dissolution of the Monasteries, King Henry VIII granted an exchange of the lordships of Badby and

Newnham for the manor of Blisworth, to Sir Edmund Knightley. The property remained in the family for the subsequent 500 years. Sir Charles Knightley was the last of the line, having inherited the estate in 1912.

The two Everdons: Little Everdon Hall was built on the site of an old manor house. Little is known of its history, except that, along with Great Everdon and the now deserted hamlet of Snorscombe in the valley, it was a medieval settlement within the parish. It is now well known as the venue of the annual horse trials.

Mentioned in AD 944 as 'Eferdun', it was recorded in the Domesday Book as 'Everdone'. The name was originally thought to mean 'hill of the wild boar', and later still it became 'Churche Everdon' before its present form. After the Norman Conquest it was held by the Bishop of Bayeux, and later, in the reign of Henry II, came into the possession of the Benedictine abbey of Bernay, in Normandy. The manor and priory of Everdon were given to the Provost and Fellows of Eton College by Henry VI in 1440, who was the founder of this seat of learning.

The church of St Mary, on a mound at Great Everdon, dominates the main street and dates from the 14th century (the font even earlier). It has a fine south doorway and was perhaps built by monks and villagers toiling together on this vast building. Basically crafted of local ironstone, which has required much restoration, the tougher oolite limestone carved for the windows has better withstood the weathering of passing years.

Fawsley: Fawsley Hall is an ornate mansion standing above the site of deserted settlements on low scarps and banks. It has had a chequered history, dating back to Henry VIII. Sir Edmund Knightley, who died in 1542, commissioned the building, where successive generations have left their mark.

21

In the Second World War, much damage was inflicted by troops stationed there, and it was later put to use as a timber factory, resulting in further dereliction. The property has now been saved by a private owner and sensitively restored to its former glory.

The renowned master, 'Capability' Brown, landscaped the extensive parkland, reflected today in this exquisite panorama. Within the park, Charles I came to hunt deer, and was brought tidings of Cromwell's advance.

Not far from Badby Wood is the sad rubble of the Dower House, built in the 16th century for the dowager Lady Ursula Knightley, widow of Sir Edmund. It was this lady who planted an avenue of cherry trees for her feathered friends.

There is a dire tale of warning relating to the Dower House:

'A sinister horseman dressed in green
On a wild grey horse may still be seen
He blows his horn but makes no sound
As he wildly gallops all over the ground
The omen of death he's said to be
So stay indoors on New Year's Eve!'

The isolated church of St Mary, standing on a slight rise surrounded by a ha-ha, dates back to around 1209, and was probably built on the site of an early Saxon church. The many treasures include outstanding stained glass, marble monuments and memorials of the Knightley family.

The box pews and carvings are of interest as well as the intricately carved panels removed from the Dower House, illustrating perhaps a touch of medieval treason in the interpretation, in the reign of Richard III, of the old nursery rhyme 'Hey Diddle Diddle, The Cat and The Fiddle'.

Newnham and Upper Weedon

(Nene Way – Little Everdon to Upper Weedon)

Introduction: From Little Everdon, the Nene Way clings to the south side of the valley till it comes to the larger community of Weedon on the colourful Grand Union Canal. This circular walk however begins in the ancient village of Newnham, partly surrounded by old ridge and furrow meadows. Although this means that it covers a short part of the route walked in Walk One, it does enable the walker to return to Newnham along the other side of the beautiful river Nene, past Dodford Mill. The range of Northamptonshire Heights is to the west and includes Arbury Hill at 734 ft, flanked by Big Hill (705 ft) on one side and Sharman's Hill (700 ft) on the other.

Distance: The entire circuit is about 5.5 miles. Nene Way section 2 miles. Suitable gear in inclement weather may be needed when negotiating the sequence of large arable fields, where the path is usually well defined but may prove muddy underfoot. OS Landranger series 1:50 000 map 152 Northampton & Milton Keynes.

Refreshments: On the green at Newnham is The Romer Arms. There are no pubs in Little Everdon, but plenty of choice of taverns etc in Weedon Bec. This is a very rural area and consequently sparse in services.

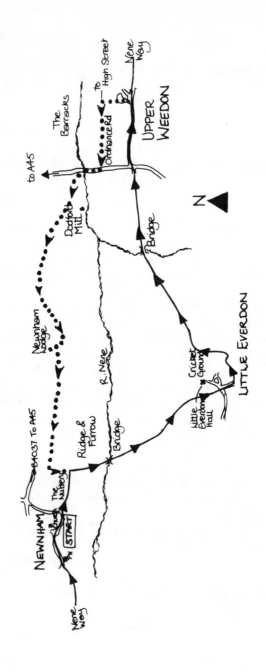

NENE WAY

The Barracks

to A45

Dalton's Mill

to High Street

Ordnance Rd

UPPER WEEDON

NENE WAY

Bridge

N

Newnham Lodge

B4037 To A45

R. Nene

Ridge & Furrow

Bridge

Cricket Ground

LITTLE EVERDON

Little Everdon Hall

NEWNHAM

The Nuttery

START

NENE WAY

How to get there: Newnham is on the B4037 between the A361 and the A45, south of Daventry. The walk begins at the church.

Nen Way – Little Everdon to Upper Weedon: The second section of the Way starts at Little Everdon, part way through the circular walk, and follows the circular walk to Upper Weedon, before continuing through Weedon with Walk Three.

The Walk: Begin the circular walk at the church of St Michael and All Angels in Newnham village. Join the Nene Way and follow it through the churchyard on the sunken path. Go down the narrow leafy lane to the T junction and turn left to The Nuttery, a commercial nut farm.

Follow the Nene Way posts over the fields to charming Little Everdon Hall, laid out in an expanse of parkland. The jumps of the Everdon Horse Trials are a permanent fixture. Skirt the Hall, head for the yard and exit by stone steps cunningly fashioned in the handsome wall. The Old House opposite is 17th century and one of only a few houses in this tiny hamlet. **(Rejoin the Nene Way here from Walk One.)** Facing uphill in Little Everdon (towards Great Everdon), walk a short distance to the last house, and garden, to a stile on the left side and Nene Way sign.

Through the trees of the Hall parkland, the thatched cricket pavilion and pitch create a truly traditional setting, and the perfect backdrop for the Sunday afternoon game of English gentlemen!

The bridleway follows a direct line into the hollow, over the bridge and up again, to a road T junction. Go straight over to the outskirts of Upper Weedon and up the hill, where Oak Street is in front. For the next section of the **Nene Way**, continue with Walk Three.

On this walk, the road curves down to Princes Close, a cul-de-sac to the right of Myrtle Cottage. In the left-hand corner the path leads between the hedges to Ordnance Road, which is just a worn grass track. Turn left away from the village. The Depot (Georgian Barracks) is almost opposite. A diversion of further interest may be taken by turning right from the first footpath on to Ordnance Road (instead of left) and through to the High Street. Climb the bank to the boatyard basin on the Grand Union Canal, a busy and colourful locality dotted with shops, with a variety of moored or passing boats, which was the original short arm of the canal into the Military Depot, later blocked.

Return to Ordnance Road and the route of the walk and at the dirt farm track, go over the bridge and narrow river. In a few yards, go through the gate on the left to a quiet path over two fields to the Everdon/Weedon road (off the A45).

Cross to the other side where the footpath sign directs you over the field diagonally towards a hut, and briefly keeps to the lane on the private land to Dodford Mill. In about 100 yards on the right, a waymark points again diagonally to the far hedgerow. In the corner, pass to the next field where rolling vistas open up. Keep to the headland, with the masts of Daventry and the A45 traffic on the horizon. Over an undulating field next, and the ruin of the stone barn in the depression, coming to a corner and footbridge with very steep banks.

Forward now, keeping the hedge to the left and walking parallel with the minor road B4037, to the dip and through the hedge, where the path is clearly marked, heading for the treetops and visible roof of Newnham Lodge. At the curve, follow the track and change to having hedge on the right, turning toward a post and rail fence, not yet crossing but staying alongside to the brow of the hill, on a light sandy soil.

On the far side of the valley, Everdon Hall is partially hidden in a veil of trees, and in the distance looms the high plateau of Everdon Hill and Badby Wood.

In the next field, with hedge, then fence, to the right, pass from arable to pastures on the 'permitted path', where walkers are asked to respect the landowner's preferred route.

The spire of the church at Newnham peeps through the trees ahead and there are magnificent views all around. In the second pasture, a stile and waymark point to the road, but turn downhill instead, making for a lone telegraph pole in the ancient ridge and furrow, parallel to the rookery. Drop to a lower level to rejoin the Nene Way at the gateway adjacent to The Nuttery. Retrace your steps back into the village.

Historical Notes

Newnham: King Canute, in a Saxon charter of 1021, is recorded as granting land at Newnham to Monk Aevic for five hides. A number of finds have been unearthed of skeletons, weapons, numerous brooches and ornaments, from an early burial site in the vicinity. The jewellery has been placed in the Northampton Museum.

The battlemented tower and spire of the church dedicated to St Michael and All Angels are from the 15th century, although parts of the edifice are purported to date from the 12th century. The unique bell tower is supported by three arches forming a porch, where the ropes passed through holes in the floor and were rung in the open porchway.

The pub, The Romer Arms, is named after a lawyer and local benefactor, Romer Williams of Welsh origin, who resided at the Hall in the late 1800s. Several of the dwellings have herringbone designs in the stonework, and the village is surrounded to a large extent by old ridge and furrow meadows, the common fields being enclosed by an Act of Parliament in 1764.

Little Everdon: Medieval earthworks in the vicinity suggest a larger settlement than at present. The common fields of both parishes, Little and Great Everdon, were enclosed by an Act of Parliament in 1763.

Upper Weedon: The name Weedon derives from 'hill with a temple or sacred place', and has played an important role in history. The Royal Military Barracks, later recognised as the Ordnance Depot, was constructed in 1803, following an Act of Parliament allowing for an extensive arsenal and barracks for soldiers.

It was thought to be a safe haven for George III, who was to take up residence with his entourage in the Royal suite of three pavilions in the event of the anticipated Napoleonic invasion in the 1800s. The town was ideally situated in the heart of the country and as far as possible from the coast. The short arm from the main canal was protected by a portcullis in case of waterborne attack, and the powder magazines and barracks for the regiments stood safely within the walls. In 1824, the water-way was put to use in transporting troops from Ireland, when 28 boats used this very route.

The complex now takes on a comparatively mundane role to that of the past, housing more prosaic industries, under private ownership. It may be seen across the narrowing valley of the Nene.

Dodford Mill: Once used by the villagers of Newnham for grinding their corn, Dodford Mill now stands in isolation on the spot where there has been a mill for more than a millennium.

Nether Heyford and the Grand Union Canal

(Nene Way – Weedon to Nether Heyford)

Introduction: This circular walk begins at Nether Heyford, where you will find one of the largest village greens in the country, covering more than five acres. Then it's over the Grand Union Canal and across open countryside to Stowe Nine Churches and the lovely church of St Michael, where the ground drops away sharply to give wonderful views towards Daventry. Down into the valley, the walk returns to Nether Heyford along the willow-lined towpath of the Grand Union Canal. Or you may wish to make a detour to the village of Flore, over the river Nene, in which case you can return to Nether Heyford along this section of the Nene Way.

Distance: From Weedon Bec to Nether Heyford on the Nene Way 2.5 miles. Circular walk from Nether Heyford and returning along the towpath approximately 5 miles. The walk may be extended to include Flore if preferred, as an alternative to the canalside. OS Landranger series 1:50 000 map 152 Northampton & Milton Keynes.

Refreshments: In Flore, The White Hart and The Royal Oak are both a little distance away on the High Street though not directly en route. Pubs in Heyford are The Olde Sun in Middle Street and The Forester's Arms close to the green, in addition to a patisserie and coffee shop nearby, plus several small shops.

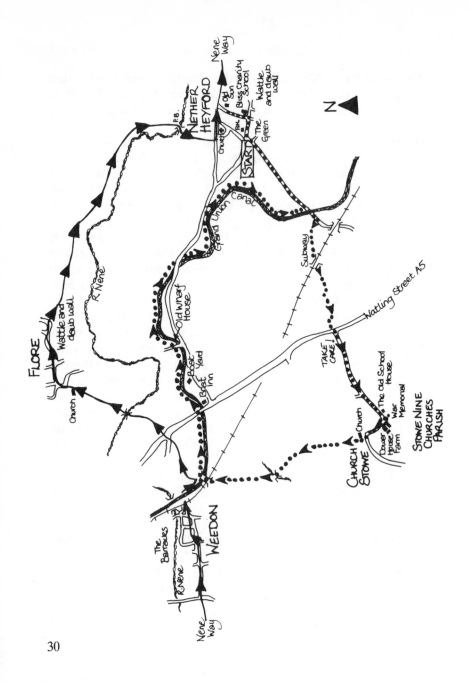

N

FLORE

Wattle and daub wall

Church

R. Nene

NETHER HEYFORD

P.B.

Church

Old Sun

Bliss Charity School

Wattle and daub wall

P.H.

START

The Green

Grand Union Canal

Oldwharf House

Boat Yard

Boat Inn

Subway

Watling Street A5

TAKE CARE!

The Old School House

War Memorial

Church

Dower House Farm

CHURCH STOWE

STOWE NINE CHURCHES PARISH

The Barracks

R. Nene

WEEDON

Nene Way

Nene Way

How to get there: Nether Heyford is situated about 1 mile south of the A45 from Northampton to Daventry, turning off at Upper Heyford. The walk begins at Furnace Lane near the green.

Nene Way – Upper Weedon to Nether Heyford: In Upper Weedon, with Oak Street ahead, follow the Nene Way past The Old Priory and around the bend to New Croft. At the cul-de-sac, first left, there is a path threading through the back gardens of the housing estate, giving an occasional glimpse of the brick Barracks in the distance. Cross where New Croft meets Manor Road, to the footpath known locally as The Whettles and over the Weedon road to South Street, which eventually merges with Church Street at the five-arched blue brick viaduct carrying the railway line.

Go through the churchyard and at the foot of the embankment are more than 30 'sleeper' steps to canalside moorings only (no footpath). Carry on along Puddle Bank and under the aqueduct. Immediately to the right, mount the steps to the top and turn left at the waterside to follow the towpath, where a lone residence, Weedon Wharf, stands on the far side. Continue beside the sluggish flow to the brick bridge, as the canal briefly narrows, and up the slope to the track on the bridge (the circular walk returns here) and down towards the A5 which is in sight.

Cross the A5 with great care, to the fingerpost. Continue to follow the Nene Way next to the stream and over the wooden bridge, to the main river and dilapidated barn to the low lying area called The Lakes, and to All Saints church at Flore.

From the gates, bear right in front of the school to traverse Nether Lane and Kings Lane, on the perimeter of the village. Depart near to the Scouts hall for Nether Heyford, between ancient thatched wattle and daub walls and an iron kissing-gate just set back from the bend.

Passing the derelict Heyford Mill, with Upper Heyford on

the skyline, climb over about a dozen stiles with Nene Way markers to reach a good bridge with 'chimney-pot' treads. Turn sharp right round the new estates, the Manor House and church of St Peter and St Paul to Middle Street in Nether Heyford. The Nene Way continues in Walk Four.

The Walk: Begin at Furnace Lane in Nether Heyford, adjacent to the green. Walk down to the bridge which spans the Grand Union Canal, almost opposite Wharf Farm. On the right, a green fingerpost points to a short path alongside an electricity box and a hummocky field. Go over the little bridge, bearing left around the edge of the field and through a narrow horseshoe-shaped subway under the main railway line. Take the bosky passage beside the stream over old meadows, and watch for the gap in the crumbling red brick walls and the iron ladder-stile, keeping left along the bottom of the embankment.

Take extra care in crossing the A5 and the relentless pulse of traffic (there are compensations to follow!). Go straight up the quiet lane, with the abandoned tramway in the dip. Look back to see the 'Lighthouse' (Express Lift Tower) at Northampton, and nearer, the re-opened limestone quarry at the former Stowe Iron Works.

A tall lamp-post, lane to the Manor and roadside sign 'Stowe Nine Churches, Church Stowe' announces the joint hamlets of this peaceful community, which has an intriguing history.

Follow round the bend, graced by The Old School House, yard and war memorial to Dower House Farm and the elegant stone Wyndham House, all reflecting the same serene ambience. On the other side is the lovely lychgate to St Michael's church, blessed with a sturdy Saxon tower and a small Norman north doorway, harbouring treasures of fine marble inside.

The fingerpost 'to Weedon' is next to the lofty churchyard, where the ground slides away to a steep drop and a breathtaking landscape over toward Daventry. Descend gradually to the valley floor and go over the solid bridge (which may be partially hidden in the hedgerow) across the brook. Walk round the edge of the field to a track over the canal bridge, where the Nene Way comes up the bank from Weedon.

To avoid the hazards of the A5 again, go down the right bank to the towpath past Canal Cottage, a waterpoint for boats and under the noisy road. The Narrow Boat Motel and marine yard soon come into view and in about a hundred yards, a gap in the hedge is the cue for the footpath to Flore. If you decide to visit Flore, follow the Nene Way back to Nether Heyford.

Otherwise, remain on the towpath, passing a chain of affluent homes with landscaped gardens and compact orchards, some with boats on the moorings. In summer, verdant growth carpets these banks, overhung with weeping willows, creating a picturesque scene at every twist and turn of the water. Austere farms, barns, brick and mellowed stone bridges unfold, with sometimes flat meadows or arable slopes which sweep away to the horizon. A fetching cottage, snuggled in the lee of the bank, has a post proclaiming 'Braunston 11 miles' for those who might feel the need to know!

Continue on the winding towpath to return to Nether Heyford.

Historical Notes

Weedon: St Peter's church in Lower Weedon, strangely sandwiched between the canal escarpment bolstering the waterway and the railway line, has a weathervane in the shape of a goose – and thereby hangs a tale.

In the days of the Mercian kings, King Ethelred appointed his niece, St Werburgh, to oversee the nunnery here, which had been converted from the royal palace. Wild geese were proving troublesome, decimating the vital crops and causing food shortages in the community. St Werburgh is said to have banished the marauding birds from the parish by prayer, and legend has it that none have ever appeared on the lands since.

33

Remembered by a stained glass window in the church, she was buried at Chester Cathedral.

The Grand Union Canal: Although the Oxford Canal had been in existence since 1778, carrying cargoes from the Midlands via Banbury, and on to Oxford and the Thames at Brentford, by 1790 plans were afoot for another route to London. An Act of Parliament, to which George III affixed his assent in 1793, enabled the Grand Union Canal Company to proceed with the ambitious construction of a further route bearing their name.

The northern end linked with the Great Oxford Canal at Braunston, and a complete waterway was at last officially opened in 1805, which stretched all the way to the city.

This marathon undertaking was beset with a number of problems resolved after many trials and tribulations. One stumbling block was a missing link at Blisworth, where a primitive horse-drawn railway was operating, causing precious time to be squandered in unloading each boat, reloading to the wagons and repeating the exercise on the Stoke Bruerne side. Blisworth Tunnel, opened in 1805, is 3,065 yards in length and finally connected the two arms, where 'leggers' then walked the boats through, lying on their backs on boards, treading the roof – a neat solution before the days of powered boats.

Another enormous problem awaiting a solution, on the border with Buckinghamshire, was solved when an aqueduct, the Iron Trunk, was erected on piers to carry the canal over the Great Ouse Valley. This novel idea was the brainchild of William Jessop, the engineer responsible for the project, but it collapsed in 1808 and was temporarily replaced by a wooden trough, before completion in its present form in 1810. It was inscribed 1811–1821 on the parapet when later under repair.

The unique Trunk, 101 ft long and 15 ft wide, is now a popular attraction and an easy walk from Cosgrove (see Northamptonshire Rambles by same author), enabling the walker not only to wander beside the water, but also to pass beneath it by a singular 'cattle-creep' which is worthy of investigation.

Flore: Flore was already established at the time of the Domesday Book, with a manor and mills. It was set beside the turnpike road and was probably once spread over the lower valley slopes, as indicated by the mounds in that area.

Nether Heyford: Furnace Lane, at the start of the Circular Walk, takes its name from the locality of three blast furnaces operating here until 1891. This was a hive of industrial activity where the ironworks utilised the local ironstone for the making of steel, and for the production of clay for bricks and tiles in nearby yards.

Sports, fairs, fetes and events are now held on the spacious village green, but until 1924 the annual grazing rights were much sought after and bid for by an unusual method. A pin was stuck into a burning candle to signal the beginning of the proceedings, which were concluded when the pin fell out! Just across the road, an ancient wattle and daub wall remains, though no longer with the original thatch, but topped by a row of tiles.

Around the corner in Middle Street, The Olde Sun is an attractive pub, with a colourful selection of old grinding implements and machinery on display on the extensive forecourt. Set on the site of an early monastery, it is now a listed building. Close to the green is The Forester's Arms, also fashioned from Northamptonshire sandstone.

Brasses to the Maunsell family, who occupied the manor of Heyford from the 14th century, are in the church of St Peter and St Paul. After their downfall, when Sir Walter was involved in rebellion, the manor was confiscated by the Crown. The property was then purchased by Sir Frances Morgan, a Judge on the King's Bench, and it is believed that it was he who pronounced the sentence of death on Lady Jane Grey. He later committed suicide in 1556, and the family memorial is also in the church. The Manor was subsequently ravaged by the Parliamentarians during the Civil War and left in ruins. A new Manor was later built in Nether Heyford in the 18th century.

William Bliss was a wine merchant and native of the village, who left his mark by bequeathing the sum of £400 to build and maintain the Bliss Charity School. Facing the green, it was endowed in 1674, opened in 1683, and rebuilt in 1880, where boys and girls were taught in separate classes.

In a more modern vein, the local folk are proud to have financed and built the present village hall entirely by their own voluntary labour. It was opened by Viscount Althorp in 1960.

Stowe: Since medieval times the village has been known as Stowe, meaning 'holy place'.

Stories abound as to the 'nine churches'. One records the simple explanation of nine churches being visible from the hilltop, whilst another tells of succeeding frustration and failure by the lord of the manor and his men to build the original church. The site of the church was said to be near a magical fairy ring, and for eight days the foundations were mysteriously filled in under the cover of darkness. On the ninth night, a monk stayed beside the stone blocks and no further mishap occurred, so the work could continue!

The superb elevated church of St Michael has a Saxon west tower, a small Norman north doorway and is guardian of notable marble monuments.

The ironworks, with a blast furnace, was first opened in 1866 and suffered mixed fortunes over the ensuing years, until it was more recently reopened as a quarry for building stone.

Kislingbury
(Nene Way – Nether Heyford to Upton)

Introduction: On leaving Nether Heyford, the Nene Way passes through a series of peaceful meadows. Though not actually touching the village of Bugbrooke, up on the hill, a short detour could easily be made if the walker has an interest in Quakerism. Bugbrooke was once a centre of the sect, where members were imprisoned for their faith in the 17th century. The Meeting House was at Quakers Cottage, in the High Street.

This fascinating circular walk is centred on the historic village of Kislingbury, and can be divided into two short rambles if required. It was near this pretty village that General Fairfax and Oliver Cromwell camped before the battle of Naseby in 1645. Today there are still old thatched cottages and a lovely 14th century church to be seen. There were mills at regular intervals along the river Nene and Upton Mill, now a private residence, provides a particularly pleasant spot for a walk with its stream and nearby lake where birds swoop and call.

Distance: Nether Heyford to Kislingbury on the Nene Way 2.2 miles. Circular walk giving two circuits of 3.5 miles (east) and 2.5 miles (west). OS Landranger series 1:50 000 map 152 Northampton & Milton Keynes.

Refreshments: In Kislingbury only – The Sun, The Old Red

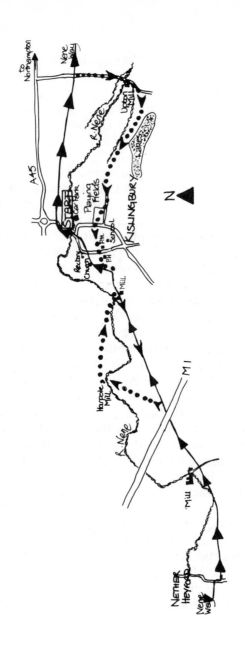

to Northampton

Nene Way

A45

R. Nene

Upton Mill

N

START
Car Park

Playing Fields

School

P.H.
P.H.

Rectory
Church

KISLINGBURY

Mill

Harpole Mill

R. Nene

M1

Mill

NETHER HEYFORD

Nene Way

38

Lion and The Cromwell Cottage Restaurant, near to the bridge.

How to get there: Kislingbury, 4 miles west of Northampton, is on the B4525 Northampton to Banbury road, turning south from the A45. There is a riverside car park at Beech Lane.

Nene Way – Nether Heyford to Upton: On this fourth section, leave Nether Heyford from Watery Lane on a track between two houses. The path then turns off to the left to cross about eight fields. One of the stiles has been modified with an unusual dogflap, which enables pets to pass under the 'paddle' where stockproof fencing might otherwise block the way. Unfortunately there is now no trace of the site of the Roman building that once stood in the valley, just a distant view of Glassthorpe Hill, a deserted hamlet.

Coming back to the river again, there is a pleasant approach to the bustling Heygate's Mill as the smell of milling corn wafts across from the bulky premises. Keep to the public footpath and cross the service road which leads directly into the industrial site and go forward beneath the ceaseless ribbon of traffic on the M1.

Emerging to quieter pastures, head for Kislingbury over fields steeped in history, if only they could tell the tale! Cross the stile and follow the Nene Way markers along Mill Road, where sheep used to be dipped in the river, turning sharp left at The Sun into Church Lane.

Walk toward the squat tower and spire of the church of St Luke, which contains an octagonal font of great age, and out through the gates of the churchyard, past the ancient bulging mud wall. Pause for a moment to admire the illustrated village signpost. The Old Rectory occupies a position of importance here and is a striking building.

Cross the road and follow it around the curve to the bridge. Here is the riverside car park at Beech Lane, and you now follow the course of the circular walk as far as Mill Lane at Upton. Then continue at Walk Five.

The Walk: From the riverside car park at Beech Lane, join the Nene Way and go over the wooden footbridge. Look over the parapet to the parallel narrow road bridge, with its quaint single cutwater.

A green fingerpost 'to Duston' stands next to the oak Nene Way post. Follow the appropriate waymarks (not the parallel track next to the stile) over the next seven fields, which include an iron ladder-stile, stream and bridge. The path is well defined and leads toward massed trees in the distance, which effectively cloak Quinton House School.

Once again, the landmark of the 'lighthouse' rears up from the horizon, as the path runs next to a rich stone wall with a splendid archway, complete with a snug door to restrain peeping. The farmyard is next, to emerge at Mill Lane and some brick cottages. Here the Nene Way carries on (see Walk Five) to meet the Upton Way and over to the derelict site of Duston Mill.

To continue the walk, turn downhill past large sheds and a view of Hunsbury Hill (site of an Iron Age fort) to Upton Mill, a private residence. The path skirts round the back of the house and passes over tumbling water. Between the two iron gates, in this quiet meadow, stand several beautiful willows, some with split trunks.

Turn right alongside the stream, walking between the lakes and heed the warning 'deep quarry workings'. Birdwatchers, particularly those keen on wildfowl, might find this a fascinating area, where the honking and calling of birds float over the tranquil fields, changing from season to season.

The track is in good order and patches of tough marsh grass edge it in places. After the iron handgate, at the playing fields, turn in and make for the village, joining the concrete path back to the lane, which is bordered by a row of fine homes. Return to the car park, just out of sight beyond the bend to complete the first circular walk.

To extend the walk for another 2½ miles, on leaving the recreational park, look out for the lovely stone house, lamp-post, and adjacent path (with a cycle sign). This winds past lofty pine trees, the school, and glimpses of both modern and old thatched dwellings tucked away behind walls, where the walker must be prepared to step high over the superb stone slab stile, before reaching the High Street next to The Old Red Lion.

Cross the road and on the corner of Starmers Lane, pick up the Nene Way again (reverse direction) past the Old Dairy, into Church Lane and Mill Road, with the thatched ironstone building of the Sun public house at the apex.

Double back around this point and further along is the neat Baptist church of 1828, facing the meadows, where the mill has been ingeniously converted to a fireplace factory. The path continues forward past the new housing estate and last bungalow, over several fields, with Heygate's Mill at Bugbrooke looming over the motorway.

At the last hedge before the underpass and leaving the Nene Way again, branch off to the right, veering away from the traffic, to the sparse remains of Harpole Mill across the fields.

Turn sharp right here and follow the path beside the winding water and weir, toward the clutch of buildings at Kislingbury Mill and over the bridge at Mill Road.

Rejoin Church Lane as before to return to the bridge at Beech Lane.

Historical Notes

Heygate's Mill (Nene Way): fulfils the tradition of corn milling on the site where water-mills have been in place for hundreds of years. It is one of the few working mills surviving these days, on the river Nene.

Kislingbury: Known as 'Cifelingebeire' in the Anglo-Saxon era, Kislingbury later became better known for the connection with the battle of Naseby in 1645, when General Fairfax camped his army of Parliamentarians nearby to await the arrival of Oliver Cromwell, who is said to have tethered his horses in the churchyard on the night prior to the conflict.

The Old Rectory was constructed of local ironstone in the 18th century and attributed to Francis Smith of Warwick, who was the architect for Lamport rectory and Cottesbrooke Hall. The nearby stout barn, edging the road, is topped by a cupola and has more than 1,300 nesting boxes for pigeons. These birds formed an essential part of the villagers' diet in medieval times, and a large number of dovecotes have survived in the county, many in good order.

Upton: Quinton House School, the original Upton manor, was purchased by Sir Thomas Samwell in 1600 from the Knightleys of Fawsley. They had held the manor since 1419, when they banished the tenants to enable substantial sheep farming, from which the family fortunes were assured. Consequently, the community dispersed and, as in many places, only vague traces now remain on the ground. This lost village is designated a scheduled Ancient Monument.

The White Lady of Upton is said to haunt the grounds on a moonlit midnight! Tablets and monuments in St Michael's church next to the school, commemorate Thomas Samwell and the Knightleys.

Northampton

(Nene Way – Upton to Northampton)

Introduction: Quitting the peaceful pastures, the Nene Way changes dramatically as it wends its way through the districts of St James and Cotton End at Northampton, where the river and canal run side by side for a while. The Northampton arm of the Grand Union Canal ends here at lock 17 in the locality of the early depots and berthing docks.

This is a circular walk which provides an opportunity to discover more of this ancient town's history. It visits Delapre Abbey, founded in the 12th century and with superb ornamental gardens and parkland, before reaching the 13th century Eleanor Cross. Only three of these royal memorials have survived to the present day and this alone makes the walk notable. However, the route then goes through Hunsbury Hill Country Park, with its Iron Age hill fort. A great deal of work has been done to recreate the old ironstone industry of this area and the railway that served it, which makes a fascinating diversion. The walk then joins the Nene Way to return to South Bridge.

Distance: Kislingbury to Northampton on the Nene Way about 3.5 miles. The circular walk is approximately 5 miles. OS Landranger series 1:50 000 map 152 Northampton & Milton Keynes, or local town map.

Refreshments: Coffee shop at Superstore, Ransome Road. The

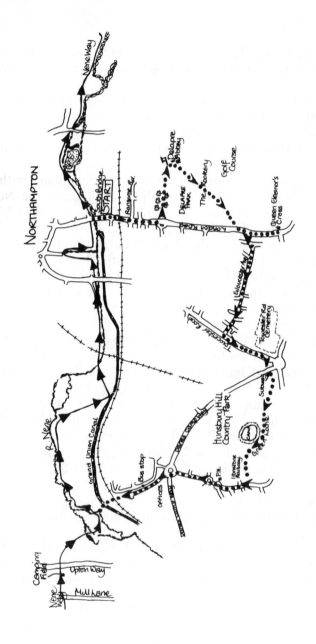

NORTHAMPTON

Nene Way

South Bridge
START

Rangore Rd.

London Road

P.R.S.

DELAPRE PARK

Delapre Abbey

The Rookery

Golf Course

Queen Eleanor's Cross

R. Nene

Grand Union Canal

Gloucester Way

Towcester Rd. Cemetery

Hunsbury Hill Country Park

Bus stop

Offices

Ironstone Railway

P.H.

Great Roune

Subway

Camp

Camping Field

Upton Way

Nene Way

Mill Lane

44

Nene Valley Retail Park and centre beyond, on the Towcester Road, is a useful comfort stop. There are also many town pubs.

How to get there: Local buses on main roads and from Briar Hill and Hunsbury Hill Country Park to town centre. From town centre follow Bridge Street down one-way system to South Bridge at Cotton End. The walk starts at South Bridge.

Nene Way – Upton Mill Lane to Northampton South Bridge: For this fifth section from Upton Mill Lane, the Nene Way goes on to cross the dual width of the Upton Way (A45) just below the filling station and hotel, going down Duston Mill Lane directly opposite, to the abandoned mill site. Just beyond the second bridge, go over the stile to the left (where the circular walk joins the Way on its return journey), to follow the waymarks through the environs of the county town, via the industrial areas.

Follow the river over the remaining thin wedge of water meadows, as far as the hump-backed canal bridge (though not crossing), to double back and cross an iron railed bridge over the river and under the railway viaducts. Over the bank topped by boulders is the shopping complex, with spacious car parking. The cinder track then passes below the Towcester Road to the derelict gasworks and turns away from the main waterway beside the short channel, to the massive silos at Carlsberg Brewery and the landscaped verges, to South Bridge. To continue on the Nene Way, turn to Walk Six.

The Walk: From the point where the Nene Way reaches South Bridge turn to the right on the bridge, by the conglomeration of warehouses that edge the road, and go over the rail crossing at Cotton End, at the start of London Road (A508). Cross Ransome Road and very soon a stone wall surrounds the premises of the Northampton Society of Model Engineers, with the rich brown stone of Delapre Lodge on the corner.

45

Turn left here to wander along beneath the towering avenue of limes through the park to the formal gardens and Delapre Abbey, formerly the County Records Office. Cross the greensward of the park back towards the road, past The Rookery and skirting the golf course. Head for the right-hand corner to continue under the belt of trees (which may be messy underfoot in wet weather) to meet the roadside pavement.

A little further on, set high on the bank and steps well above road level, the Eleanor Cross is a reminder of the sad story of Edward I, who mourned his beloved wife, Eleanor, and commissioned this poignant memorial after her death.

Cross here and retrace your steps to Gloucester Road on the left, a quiet tree-lined road. Follow it to the very end, turning left into Towcester Road. On the far side from the cemetery, look for the start of the cycle track in the tiled subway under Danes Camp Way, thus avoiding the intricate roundabout.

Once out of the subway the path follows the old green lane for a while, to enter Hunsbury Hill Country Park. Carry on over the crest at Hill Fort and eventually over the railway line through to the car park and Hunsbury Hill railway and engine sheds.

Exit to Hunsbury Hill Road and turn right, past The Viking public house and a small parade of shops and down the hill to the roundabout at Danes Camp Way. Cross with caution to a large factory unit occupying one corner of the entrance to the lane, which deteriorates as it runs beside tall poplars, separating the industrial and residential estates. Through The Causeway gap, the nearby bus stops on both sides of the road may be handy to return to town.

Go over the railway and canal bridges and, just before the river, the track meets the Nene Way at the bottom of Duston Mill Lane. Turn right and complete the trail, with St James' in the distance, by following the Nene Way back to South Bridge.

Historical Notes

Northampton was an area of rapid expansion in the 1970s and 1980s, along with Milton Keynes to the south and Corby to the east, at a time when Birmingham and London were already burdened by industry and a wider economic region was envisaged.

The footwear industry was most prolific in the 19th century when a revolution in working had been taking place. Before 1850 boots and shoes were made by hand and the outworkers cobbled in their homes or, frequently, in sheds in their backyards. When mechanisation and factory systems came into force, workers resented the loss of choice in taking in work. Rows of terraced houses sprang up to accommodate the factory workers and perhaps offered better living conditions for some, although many grieved the loss of their independence.

Gradually the manufacture of hose and lace ceased, and in the next century cheap imports of footwear caused many firms to close or diversify to other commodities. Nowadays, a more commercial slant has come to the fore, when banking services have become established in the commercial sector.

Warehousing and distribution centres have sprung up, as the Midlands location is ideally placed in the midst of a vast network of far reaching skeins of motorways, thus facilitating the success of allied freight operations. Food processing and technology have advanced mightily in recent years and all these combined newer industries have given a changing face to the county town and its satellite estates.

The Express Lift Tower, commonly called 'The Lighthouse', standing on the site of the medieval abbey of St James, is a landmark for miles around and can be seen from many points along the Nene Way. At 418 ft, the tower is the testing base for the lift manufacturer and is occasionally open to the public in summer.

Carlsberg Brewery: Was it by chance that the gigantic Carlsberg company chose to build this major brewery on the very spot settled by a 9th century Danish community? Modern technology, encompassed by stunning industrial architecture, has drawn attention to this enterprise, which earned a design award in 1975. The complex business of brewing and packaging is carried out on these premises as well as in Denmark, for this product which is recognised all over the world.

Delapre Abbey: Originally a house of Cluniac nuns, the abbey was founded by Simon de Senlis II, Earl of Northampton in 1145. It was purchased after the Dissolution by the Tate family, who carried out considerable modifications. In turn, the Bouveries acquired the building in the 18th century and maintained their ownership until 1945. In subsequent alterations, stone coffins were discovered, some containing skeletal remains.

After the Second World War, the Northampton Borough Council bought the property, rescuing it from the verge of destruction. Miss Joan Wake, of the Northampton Record Society promoted the idea of a repository for the county archives, and carried it forward to fruition in 1958. The Record Office was to continue to occupy the premises for some years, until a purpose built Record Office was opened in May 1991, in the grounds of Wooton Hall Park.

The superb ornamental gardens enclosed behind high walls are recommended to visit, to see the topiary, thatched pavilion and the benign statue. More great trees flank the buttressed walls and spread shade over smooth lawns in summer. Horse jumps and spacious recreation grounds abound, and the entire park is isolated from the busy surrounding area by a handsome shield of mature trees.

Eleanor Cross: Eleanor of Castile, wife of Edward I, is commemorated in this striking octagonal stone cross at Hardingstone. Her funeral cortege, on its way from Harby in Nottinghamshire, where she died in 1290, stopped at a number of royal palaces and monasteries when journeying to Westminster Abbey, prior to which her heart had been laid in Lincoln Cathedral.

Four years later, her husband erected these intricately carved monuments, only three of which have survived through the centuries. It was delicately carved by artisans of the day, one of whom is recorded as William of Ireland, who received the sum of £3 6s 8d for each figure of the queen.

Hunsbury Hill Country Park is set on the top of the hill, where segments of the ditch ramparts are still visible around the ring of the Iron Age fort site, which protected the early settlers of 2,000 years ago. The Vikings, after their invasion, recognised the superior potential of the location and left traces of their occupation, now lodged in the museum.

The green lane which runs through the park is a part of the Jurassic Way, which is said to have linked the Cotswolds to the Humber in the north. Drovers of cattle used these essential routes to travel the country, and these lanes still exist in many rural areas.

Commerical quarrying of ironstone began here in 1873, although it had been a valuable resource to the early settlers in the making of tools and weapons. The ore was sent to the furnaces ½ mile away for smelting into pig iron, the wagons rolling down the hill and recovered by horses, later to be replaced by locomotives. Both the railway and the Northampton arm of the Grand Union Canal were utilised for this purpose until, by 1921, the venture became unprofitable and was scrapped.

The Ironstone Railway Trust was formed to keep alive the historical impact of this industry, and volunteers have laid the track and restored the engines and rolling stock which may be seen at the museum, open on Sundays only. The Ironstone

Trail is mapped out in a leaflet issued by Northamptonshire Countryside Services, and illustrates many points of interest, including the museum compound and locomotives, the railway tunnel airshaft, fort site and green lane route.

There are panoramic views of the low lying town and countryside from this vantage point, from slopes suitable for picnics and recreation, and a triangulation survey pillar.

Washlands Reservoir and Clifford Hill

(Nene Way – Northampton to Clifford Hill)

Introduction: Leaving South Bridge behind, the Nene Way provides a stroll along the riverside in Becket's Park, the verdant islands in the meandering river offering protection to all kinds of wildlife, away from the madding crowd. In this pretty extended backwater it is hard to believe that one is only five minutes away from the bustling town centre.

This picturesque circular walk joins the Nene Way on the far side of the A45 from Northampton, as the urban environment is left behind and the walker is once again in attractive country-side. The huge reservoir of the Washlands Scheme, a mecca for birdwatchers, and the ancient fortification of Clifford Hill are the attractions for the outward journey, and the walk then returns via the Houghtons. Little Houghton still has its 18th century stocks on the path outside the shop/post office, at the crossroads. About a hundred years ago, William Baucutt was confined to this particular form of punishment for drunkenness and ill-treating his spouse! At Great Houghton, close by on the slight southern slopes of the valley, there are views down to the reservoir below.

Distance: South Bridge to Clifford Hill on the Nene Way is 4 miles. The circular walk is 5 miles. OS Landranger series 1:50 000 map 152 Northampton & Milton Keynes.

51

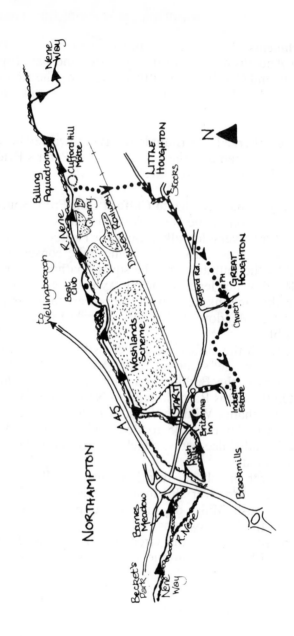

Refreshments: The Britannia Inn is at the start of the walk. Billing Aquadrome has a range of cafes and bars (open from Easter to end October). In Little Houghton, The Red Lion and in Great Houghton, The Olde Cherry Tree and The White Hart.

How to get there: The Britannia Inn is sandwiched between the Old Bedford road and the new (A428) St Peter's Bridge, east of the A45 flyover (lower level).

Nene Way – South Bridge to Clifford Hill: From South Bridge the sixth section of the Nene Way continues on the attractive paving of the riverside walk in Becket's Park, dotted with black and gold bollards. Pass Calveshome Lake conservation area, backed by the millrace, and the squat boathouse. Cross Nunn Mills Road, which leads to the big Avon Cosmetics factory and stay on the embankment, with the power station opposite, to Midsummer Meadow, with plenty of room for car parking and a toilet block.

Next reach the clubhouse and cross the bridge, going away from the strange stone chimney, connected with Anglian Water, beside the Bedford road and the bus stop at Cliftonville. On the left is Barnes Meadow Nature Reserve, managed by the Northants Wildlife Trust, which soon recedes as the path goes under the A45 to Peaches Meadow and over the Bedford road sluice gates, which control the flow of water in times of flood.

Once over the sluice, turn back to the right to follow the Nene Way loop over the footbridge and left alongside the water to Rush Mills, on the old course of the river. The Britannia Inn is opposite as you clear the underpass of the old Bedford road, where the circular walk begins. Follow it to Clifford Hill, then continue on the Nene Way with Walk Seven.

The Walk: From the road approach at the Brittania Inn, go down the bank on the far side from the pub to join the Nene Way. Continue on the Nene Way under the new road, up the grassy bank and along the ridge of the far reaching Washlands Scheme, which is a mecca for avid birdwatchers.

The Way passes over the long mesh-sided bridge, down beside the Weston Favell Barrage Gate and over the lock to the charming backwater of the Northampton Boat Club. Weston Mill has long since gone, but the sluice gates are still there near the old pools.

Deviate briefly from the river, to the end of the lane (which leads up to Weston Favell) and cross to a set back gate and stile on the right, to follow the water again, under the shimmering poplars to the boundary stile at Billing Aquadrome. Clifford Hill Lock edges the grass, and a facing post bears several directional waymarks.

Leave the **Nene Way** here and to continue the walk go over the bridges on the right, where Clifford Hill itself is partially obscured by dense clumps of trees, to the private road (public footpath). You pass the site of the former gelatine factory, of which nothing remains, and Clifford Hill House. Under the copper beech and over the filled-in cattle-grid, make for a stile on the right hand side of the lane and over two fields, keeping to the right of the pylons. The dusty road to the quarry is on the line of the dismantled railway.

Almost hidden in the fold of the hill is Little Cottage and what is left of the medieval fishponds. Turn right to Little Houghton on the road to Billing and use the pavement bordered by fine stone walls, past Little Houghton House and The Grange, with its novel 'doggy-hole' and a rather splendid view framed in the delightful archway.

At the crossroads, the stocks take up an important stance and are well tended. The church of St Mary stands opposite The Red Lion. On the way down the hill, on the left side, a fingerpost points 'to Great Houghton' and opens to good views of the Washlands Reservoir and lagoons on the floor of the valley.

Now cross ancient ridge and furrow pastures, as well as the Bedford road toward the village on the rise ahead. Approaching the old enclosure hedge, the dip indicates the line of the old medieval road and the site where Roman pottery was unearthed.

Take the path beside the closed churchyard, to the lovely Olde Cherry Tree pub in the lane of the same name. Pass April Cottage (1815) and the two thatched dwellings in Little Lane and so on to the Cross. Traces of the medieval road are faintly discernible in the field behind the bus shelter.

The steps to the war memorial are shaded by a surviving cherry tree across from the parish church of St Mary the Blessed Virgin, replacing a church from the 13th century, which has an unusual spire structure. The striking stained glass window commemorates the Queen's Silver Jubilee and illustrates the progress and genius of the British nation. It was commissioned by the Headmaster on behalf of the Great Houghton Preparatory School, established in the nearby Hall. Certainly worthy of note too, are the decorated kneelers fashioned by the parishioners, in multi-colours and a plethora of designs. Look over the surrounding churchyard wall for a glimpse of the ancient dovecote in the far corner of the rectory gardens.

The thatched White Hart is almost opposite Rectory Close, so follow this track round the wall to a field, and then diagonally to a lone willow and pond, proceeding downhill to a double fingerpost. Turn sharp left here on to the gated lane.

After the first industrial unit, join the path at the stumpy post on the right (prior to the stream and Little Norway) to the service road, Weddell Way. Cross here and bear to the right on the pavement beside a high security fence to Liliput Road roundabout. Stay on the path, which is part of the original, now neglected, road to the Britannia Inn.

Historical Notes

Northampton Castle: Practically nothing is visible of North-ampton Castle, apart from three stones mounted on an ignom-inious hump, and the re-positioned postern gate, all traces having been annihilated by the sprawling railway station yards.

Simon de Senlis, first Norman Earl of Northampton, who had fought with William the Conqueror at Hastings, was given the task of developing a fortified town and fulfilled this obliga-tion by employing masons from Normandy. Enclosing the settlement was a vast outer bailey large enough to house the garrison. The importance of the castle was recognised by Kings Henry I and Henry II, and the latter held court there at the trial of Thomas a Becket in 1164. The Archbishop of Canter-bury was committed to prison in the castle, but later escaped. Richard the Lionheart raised money here for his Third Cru-sade, and it was the chosen retreat for King John.

Partially destroyed by order of Charles II in 1662, in retalia-tion for supporting the Roundheads in the Civil War, the monarch later relented after the Great Fire of September 1675, when much of the ancient town was lost, and contributed timber from Whittlebury Forest to aid restoration. A new town arose from the ashes, embracing the churches of St Giles, St Peter and St John, which have miraculously survived to this day.

Becket's Park and Well (Nene Way): Cow Meadow was the less romantic name for this 18 acre park, now a favoured amenity with a children's playground, facilities for sport and the usual services.

It takes its present name from Thomas à Becket, Archbishop of Canterbury from 1162 to 1170, who was imprisoned in Northampton Castle after his trial. Becket's Well, on the far perimeter of the park, across the Bedford road, is said to be that from which he took a drink when he made his escape from captivity.

Washlands Scheme: Anglian Water tackled this complex project in 1976, which entailed the construction of the huge reservoir to utilise and store flood water from the river. The Bedford road sluice gates control the inward flow of water and the Weston Favell Lock regulates the outflow from the reserve. The water capacity is 500 million gallons and cost £3.8 million at completion in 1979.

Clifford Hill and Lock: Known to have been used by the Romans, who acknowledged its strategic position, by AD 800, Clifford Hill was already well established.

One of the largest mottes (mounds) in the country, it is thought to have been constructed in the 11th or 12th century, and was first mentioned in the 13th. There is no trace of the usual bailey (defence wall) though it was surrounded by a ditch. The Earl of Northampton, whose holdings were extensive, probably held control of the river crossing, which was then of vital importance, where tolls were extracted as an additional form of revenue. The top was levelled in the 17th century to make a bowling green, but the hill has since suffered slippage and returned to nature.

Standing on the spit of land at Clifford Hill Lock, a massive stone smudged by age records that 'The Hon Spencer Compton Esq' of 'trade and navigation gave this lock . . .'. Unfortunately the rest of the detail is illegible.

The celebrated county poet, John Clare, often walked this way and encapsulated his observations in his inimitable style of poetry.

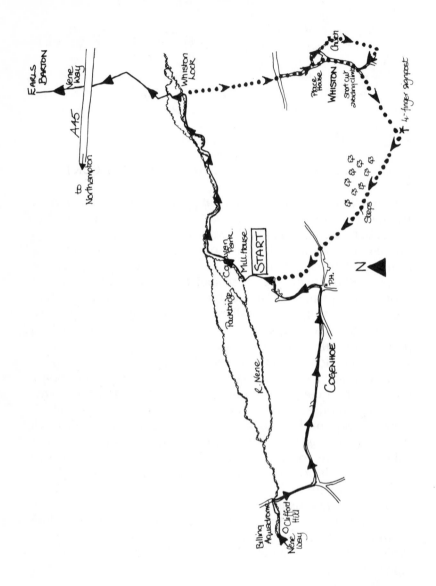

EARLS BARTON

Nene Way

A45

to Northampton

Whiston Lock

Whiston

Prace House

WHISTON Church

Short cut avoiding climb

4-finger signpost

Steps

Gowen Park

Mill House

START

Pawbridge

R. Nene

P.H.

COGENHOE

Billing Aquadrome

Nene O Clifford Way Hill

N

Cogenhoe and Whiston
(Nene Way – Clifford Hill to Whiston Lock)

Introduction: The Nene Way winds around the perimeter of Billing Aquadrome, a leisure park encompassing a spread of lakes, before continuing to the village of Cogenhoe, the start of this circular walk. The Way soon swings towards the river again, and broad stretches of the fields on the far side are frequented by 'twitchers'. Bird species such as the tufted duck, coot and lapwing, to name but a few, are here in great numbers, as well as the mallard and the heavy greylag geese who decimate some of the riverside crops. The stand of hybrid poplars are tall on the river bank, and on a sunny day cast a stately reflection on the calm water.

Sixty years ago, Whiston Lock was a popular swimming hole, where a couple of bathing huts allowed the participants to change modestly. Nowadays it is still a quiet place, undisturbed except perhaps for the boats coming and going through the lock. But as they chug away to other destinations, the stillness returns to this picturesque haven, where an alert eye might catch the darting flight of the kingfisher, or a sight of other shy creatures.

The *piece de resistance* of the walk as it cuts away from the river must surely be the church of St Mary, in a commanding position on the scarp of Combe Hill above the hamlet of Whiston. Built of grey and brown banded ashlar courses, this edifice invites closer observation and due appreciation, after the rewarding climb.

Distance: From Clifford Hill to Whiston Lock on the Nene Way about 4 miles. Cogenhoe to Whiston and return approximately 5 miles. OS Landranger series 1:50 000 map 152 Northampton & Milton Keynes.

Refreshments: Plenty of choice of bars, shops and eateries at Billing Aquadrome, where there is an entrance charge at the main gate of the park. Also The Royal Oak in Station Road, Cogenhoe.

How to get there: Cogenhoe is about 6 miles east of Northampton and easily accessible from the A45. The walk starts at Mill House.

Nene Way – Clifford Hill to Whiston Lock: The seventh section of the Nene Way now turns away from Clifford Hill lock and goes left over the little bridge, then immediately right to continue on the rim of Billing Aquadrome, on the river bank, opposite The Cliffs and the ancient mound of Clifford Hill.

Go over the wooden planked bridge not far from the old mill and up, then down the concrete ramps of the lock and along the field edge by the water. The mixed colours of the building materials of The Causeway show the amount of patchwork administered to this old bridge over the years. Go on to where the path exits at the corner to the Brafield Road.

Turn away from the bridge and walk uphill, bearing left into Cogenhoe on Station Road. Walk through the long village street as far as Church Street, bearing left where the Royal Oak is on the opposite corner. Follow the Nene Way past the green, as it weaves through a pretty alleyway and gate to an open field. The 12th century church of St Peter is on the hill as the path goes on toward Cogenhoe Mill. Join the route of the circular walk as far as Whiston Lock, then continue with Walk Eight.

The Walk: From the Green follow the Nene Way as it veers off beside the garage wall and follow it along the sinuous river bank to Whiston Lock. Here the **Nene Way** proceeds to Earls Barton. To continue on the walk, at the lock turn sharp right on to the stoned bridleway. Cross the Grendon Road at the T-junction and go straight ahead for Whiston.

For the short cut avoiding the climb on the field path to the ancient church, keep to the road round the bend as far as the post 'bridleway to Brafield'.

Otherwise, bear left past the tiny triangular patch of green to the facing handgate ahead round the corner, beside a large stone barn. The path runs initially between hedges, giving shade in summer, but may be slippery in wet conditions, shortly opening up quite steeply and giving sweeping views over the valley to Earls Barton and Doddington.

On this undisturbed prominence, just across from the venerable old church of St Mary on Combe Hill, nearby Whiston House displays spectacular chimneys and exudes an air of elegance. In the hilltop graveyard lie lichen bedecked headstones, and over the low boundary wall is an old cattle-trough, with another in the next field.

On the far side, a three pole railing makes a step-over stile in the lovely wall, where the path leads over two fields to the Castle Ashby road. As the scenery changes over the brow of the hill, the village comes into sight and reveals Castle Ashby House, built of Weldon stone, standing in its own immense grounds amidst slopes scattered with red tiled barns and farmhouses. Turning back to the right, a pleasant surprise awaits the walker, where a beautiful country home and gracious garden are hidden by the bend.

Go past the Denton turn to the next curve (meeting the shorter route) and follow the 'bridleway to Brafield' sign down the track, over a shallow ford, to a four fingered post 'bridleway to Cogenhoe'. Climb directly up the hill past a lone ash tree, to the fringe of the woodland.

A few yards into the trees, the path slightly to the left almost disappears up a very steep embankment (but do not continue forward on the more obvious trail into private land). Keep on briefly through the narrow band of trees and scrub, to emerge in the corner of a field. Go forward over the hill now, keeping to the headland strip, to where the path peters out at Jerusalem Steps. These may be a little awkward to negotiate (and are not suitable to be tackled by the infirm or young children) as they plunge down a steep escarpment, to follow a diagonal path to the far hedge, descending on a switchback verge to the Grendon Road on the outskirts of the village.

Cross here, through the gate and over the incline to follow the waymark, making for a further post and short section between garden hedges, to a high bank in Mill Lane. Turn right and rejoin the Nene Way to return to the mill.

Historical Notes

Billing Aquadrome (Nene Way): Earlier in the century the lakes were restored and landscaped after extensive gravel extraction. Although the present mill ceased operating in the 1940s, a mill was mentioned in the Domesday Book of 1086, when water-driven mills were probably built of local timber. In the planning stages, the Nene Way was to follow the public footpath which required the walker, if faithfully following it, to shin up a starkly horizontal iron ladder affixed to the stone parapet of the road bridge close to Billing Mill. As this was considered to be somewhat unseemly, the path was slightly re-routed to accommodate the less agile rambler!

Cogenhoe: In the mid 13th century the community was known as 'Kukenhoe' and it is currently pronounced 'Cook-no'. Nicholas de Cogenhoe built the church of St Peter on the hill, completed in 1290. His effigy rests there, depicted as a Crusader.

The mill bears a stone inscribed 'EW 1725', and a short sidetrack at this point will be rewarded. Go straight over the millrace, through the caravan site and bridges, on a public footpath leading to Ecton over the water-meadows, to the ancient humpbacked stone packbridge. The worn cobbles underfoot were smoothed by the passage of man and beast, when Back Brook was probably on the original watercourse, before the introduction of diversions to accommodate commercial barges and modern traffic.

In the 19th century, the church register shows many villagers in trades such as ironstone quarrying, railway labourers, waterways men and boot and shoe workers, all of which local trades have disappeared. The majority of the workforce now tend to travel further afield to pursue their various careers.

Whiston: A plaque at the side of the road records the planting of an avenue of beech trees to commemorate the Silver Jubilee in June 1977, 'unveiled' by Lord Northampton. It is also a reminder of the falling of the old line of elm trees, lost to disease.

Off to the right at Moat House, a manor of some substance once stood. Known as Place House, now only traces of the moat remain. King John is said to have used it as a hunting lodge. The Catesby family, involved in the Gunpowder Plot, inherited the estate and financed the building of the exquisite church of St Mary. The manor was demolished in 1595, when the family rebuilt it stone by stone over the valley at Ecton.

The church was built by Anthony Catesby over a period of 25 years, finally being completed in 1534, engaging masons from St Margaret's, Westminster. The elaborate tower is of banded limestone and ironstone, creating a dramatic effect, though the body of the church is in limestone only. The striking battlements and tall pinnacles soar to the sky and display the finest craftsmanship. A large number of grimacing gargoyles protrude from the facade in the guise of angels and devils, and the many monuments and benches, the font with its canopy and the stained glass windows are a delight. Altogether an elegant example of English Perpendicular architecture.

Carols by candelight take place in the Christmas season, when worshippers gather to sing and celebrate together. Each holds aloft his own flickering candle, in this lovely place where only the congregation has changed down through the centuries.

Irchester Country Park and Wellingborough

(Nene Way – Whiston Lock to Black Bridge)

Introduction: On leaving the solitude of Whiston Lock and the whispering spinney, the Nene Way arcs, in complete contrast, over the cacophonous roar of traffic below on the A45. However, it is soon hedged and peaceful again en route for Earls Barton. From there it wanders by Hardwater Mill and Great Doddington, set up on the ridge. At the Embankment at Wellingborough, swans congregate in large numbers awaiting the largesse of their benefactor at the mill.

The circular walk joins the Nene Way as it enters Irchester Country Park, a peaceful amble through mixed woodland alive with birds and small animals. The Irchester Narrow Gauge Railway Trust has a museum and compound in the park, open on Sundays. The slender spire of St Katherine's church beckons the walker on to Irchester village, and then it's on towards Black Bridge on the Nene, passing the site of a Roman walled town on the way. The walk returns along the bank of the river Nene to the Embankment at Wellingborough and past Victoria Mill, which is one of only two in the county still working.

Distance: Whiston Lock to Black Bridge on the Nene Way about 10 miles. Circular walk about 5 miles. OS Landranger series 1:50 000 map 152 Northampton & Milton Keynes.

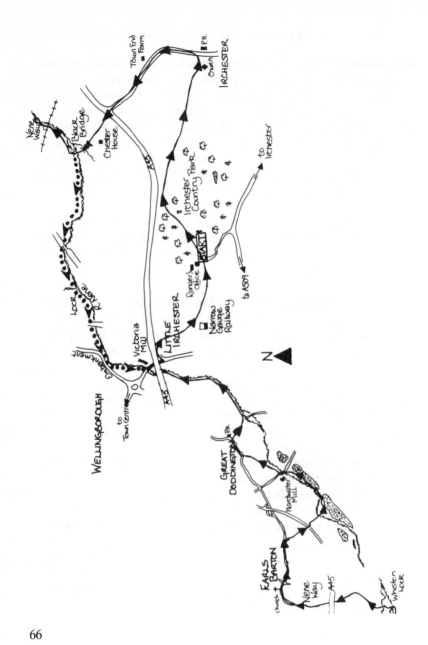

Refreshments: There are several pubs in Earls Barton, and the Apothecary coffee shop (adjoining the chemist) just across from the green, which will accept advance orders for group bookings. Mobile refreshments may operate in the Park in the summer months. In Great Doddington, The Stag's Head offers food and drink. The Carpenter's Arms in Irchester village is adjacent to and visible from the Nene Way. The Embankment at Wellingborough is near to a superstore (and filling station) with a cafe, and is about 1 mile from the town centre.

How to get there: Irchester lies to the south east of Wellingborough, off the A509. Park at the car park in Irchester Country Park, where the Countryside Rangers' Office, toilets and picnic areas can be found.

Nene Way – Whiston Lock to Black Bridge: After leaving Whiston Lock the gathering roar and smell of the A45 will perhaps urge the country lover to hurry on over the footbridge, soon then to be on Clay Lanes and shielded from the lesser road (B573) up to Earls Barton.

Crossing just before the village proper to Aggate Way, the Nene Way enters at West Street to turn right at the garage on the corner. The huge Saxon tower of All Saints' church takes pride of place as the walk goes in a forward direction up the hill to the last house, at Mill Lane.

Turn downhill, passing back over the A45. Follow the Way round and over the water past Mill House, bearing to the left and staying between the river and the series of lakes on flat land. At historical Hardwater Mill, climb the stile and walk over the narrow humpbacked bridge, watching out for the single file traffic as there is no pavement. Just on the bend, the Nene Way leaves the road for quieter pastures and takes the long, but gentle rise over a couple of fields toward farm buildings, to enter the village street of Great Doddington through a wooden swing gate.

Turn right now, along a pretty street with many detached homes and with the advantage of a valley view. Joining the main street, look for the cartwheel gate and not far beyond on the opposite side, a Nene Way oak post points downhill again to the next Mill House. (If you encounter The Stag's Head you have gone too far and need to retrace your steps a few yards.)

In the paddock, a gate lower down on the right opens to allow access to the riverside again. The Way stays on the nearside all the way to Wellingborough. As the urban area looms nearer, the path crosses a railed bridge over the weir near to the main lock and goes under the Newport Pagnell Road (A509), now leaving the river Embankment at Victoria Mill.

Go under the A45 into Little Irchester at the war memorial and left into Daniels Road. Cross Newtown Road, past the blocks of flats, to the lower end of Irchester Country Park. Walk up the cutting, past the compound of the Irchester Narrow Gauge Railway Trust, to the central block and Countryside Rangers' Office. This is the start of the circular walk where parking, picnic meadows and toilets are easily available. Follow the route of the walk to Black Bridge, then turn to Walk Nine for the next section of the Way.

The Walk: In Irchester Country Park join the Nene Way as it passes the Countryside Rangers' Office. It is waymarked throughout. It almost fleetingly touches the A45 layby, before a short diagonal field stretch, then heads back into the woodland, leaving by the north east corner up a flight of steps at the end of the quarry.

Traverse the well trodden path where, on a clear day, the spires of Rushden, Higham Ferrers, Great Harrowden and Wellingborough may be seen, in addition to the slender spire of St Katherine's ahead in Irchester village.

The stile next to the cemetery is at the top of St Katherine's Lane, next to the church. Pass Barringer Court to Main Street and The Carpenter's Arms. Turn left and stay on the roadside path, passing Town End Farm. Taking care to heed the caution sign warning of fast traffic on the A45, cross first to the central reservation, then on the the far side and down the steps. Go through the iron kissing-gate and follow a fingerpost 'footpath to Wellingborough'.

The bumpy fields next to Chester House and its squat silos are all that is left to mark the site of the Roman settlement of Chester-on-the-Water. At the bottom of the field, a pair of matching footways at Black Bridge signal the departure of **the Nene Way**, as it goes beneath the arches of the viaduct which carries the main railway line over the valley to London.

Continue on the circular walk and bear left over the bridge and keep to the bank as the river curves lazily under offending cables. Go over the footbridge, under the disused railway line and further small bridge, to the lock and wide weir. Ahead are the stark lines of the Victoria Mills and signs of industry on the outskirts of Wellingborough, with the coniferous woodland of Irchester Country Park on the horizon.

Go over the next footbridge, dykes and stile now, where this section can be muddy, to join the Embankment. This is a favourite spot in good weather. There is a playground, a paddling pool, toilet facilities and seats by the river, where fishermen are usually much in evidence.

A Nene Way sign is set on the path as it leaves the water to pass over the road bridge and under the A45, entering Little Irchester and the Park. Return to the Rangers' Office in the central area.

Historical Notes

Earls Barton (Nene Way): Established prior to the Domesday Book and recorded therein as 'Bartone', Earls Barton registers Countess Judith, niece of the Conqueror, as the land and mill owner.

At Clay Lanes between 1978 and 1980, when the construction of the A45 was imminent, a network of cropmarks of Iron Age and Roman settlements were discovered. Aerial evidence revealed late Iron Age enclosures, from which subsequent field-walking yielded coins and pottery, salvaged from the wide gravel terraces. There was also a Romano-British farmstead and field systems, with a recognisable droveway. All traces have since been erased beneath the new highway.

The ponderous Saxon tower of All Saints' church is a landmark in this thriving village. Now more than a thousand years of age, the millennium was celebrated in 1970. The square tower, unbuttressed and over 68 ft in height, replaced the wooden structure destroyed by the Danes in AD 860. The present church was extended by the Normans in the 12th century, who left their mark in the south doorway, in spiral and zigzag mouldings and other features.

Berry Mount, an impressive earthwork, is the highest point, being 170 ft above the Nene. It displays evidence of an ancient motte and bailey, with a deep ditch on the north side, perhaps the residence of a Saxon thegn (lord) whose estate netted a circle of villages.

Shoes were made here as early as the 13th century (and still are made today), then sheep farming came to the fore in the 14th and 15th centuries, when woollen cloth was produced locally. Later the natural prolific materials of the river such as rushes, were used to weave mats, baskets and similar goods. The Earls Barton Museum displays artefacts relating to the village and its history, and is situated on the premises of Barkers Shoe Factory in Station Road (opposite the green). It has limited opening times.

Hardwater Mill: On this photogenic spot once stood 'Hepdewath Mill' where, in 1309, the miller tumbled into the water and was drowned. Thomas à Becket, Archbishop of Canterbury is purported to have fled here for shelter on his escape from Northampton Castle, en route for exile in France. He later returned to England, having made his peace with Henry II, only to be murdered in Canterbury Cathedral by the King's knights in 1170.

Embankment and Mill at Wellingborough: The Embankment acts as a buffer between the river and the recreational area where many events are staged, being in close proximity to the town. The flower beds and seats under the trees attract visitors, who come for an hour or a day, to watch the water go by.

Victoria Mill, owned by Whitworths, is one of the two working mills in the county. Built in 1866, this site was ideally placed for the convenience of transport by river or rail, although both these methods of transportation have now ceased owing to the closure of the line and the cessation of commercial traffic on the river.

Irchester Country Park was opened in 1971 and is owned by Northants County Council, with financial aid from the Countryside Commission. It is based on a former ironstone quarry, Wembley Pit, which took its name from Wembley Stadium. The hilly-holly nature of the land gives a clue as to the workings of the machines, forming the humps and hollows now massed with woodland and laced with some mysterious walks.

Planted in the late 1930s and early 1940s, the coniferous trees, mainly larch and pine, still make up the bulk of the compartments, but a more recent innovation of management has been the introduction of broadleaf species, which will in time change the face of the woodland. Several ponds, spawning grounds for many of the amphibious creatures, are dotted about the park. Tiny muntjac deer come to drink, along with other nocturnal animals (no fishing please!). It is a mecca for squirrels, frequently to be seen in all seasons scuttling about their daily business and of course, the ubiquitous rabbit and the less obvious hedgehog, who all have their place in the

71

nature chain. Resident woodpeckers of three kinds, tree-creepers, wrens, sparrows, visiting cross-bills, and dark rooks holding their noisy 'parliaments', are only a fraction of the birds adding to the aerial display.

A nature trail, orienteering course, organised fossiling in the quarry, guided walks and special events such as public tree planting, are some of the attractions on offer in these 200 acres throughout the year. The Park is closed only on Christmas Day. A Countryside Ranger service is available for information and leaflets and there are kite-flying and picnic meadows, a small children's playpatch, car parking and toilets. Refreshments are usually on sale on summer weekends.

The Irchester Narrow Gauge Railway Trust has a museum and compound in the lower end of the Park, with a collection of locomotives and memorabilia. It is run by devoted enthusiasts and open to visitors on Sundays only, with regular 'steaming days' advertised locally.

Irchester village: St Katherine's is a bold church of banded oolite limestone and ironstone, with a slender soaring spire of beautiful proportions, admirable by day and by night when it is often floodlit. The weathervane, in the form of a catherine wheel, represents the wheel of torture on which the saint, namesake of the church, died. Built in the 13th century, there is an oven in the north wall of the chancel, where bread was baked for the communion and for local charities. There are also traces of the 15th century wall paintings.

The early settlement of this part of the valley is reckoned to be from the Iron Age. Succeeding generations took full advantage of the river, a basic necessity in those far off days.

Chester House is close to the site of the Roman walled town of 17.5 acres, where an aerial view revealed earthworks as a series of winding lanes within a roughly rectangular area overlooking the river. Many finds have come to light, including a considerable cache of coins and a massive stone lid from a

Roman coffin, which now rests on the mound outside the Rangers' Office at the Country Park.

The later hamlet of Chester-on-the-Water is documented in 1309 as consisting of 24 tenants, villeins and cottagers, but was deserted by the 18th century, leaving only the former manor, Chester House.

The two matching footbridges at Black Bridge were constructed to replace the dilapidated crossing at the inception of the Nene Way, and have non-slip surfaces and easy access for walkers.

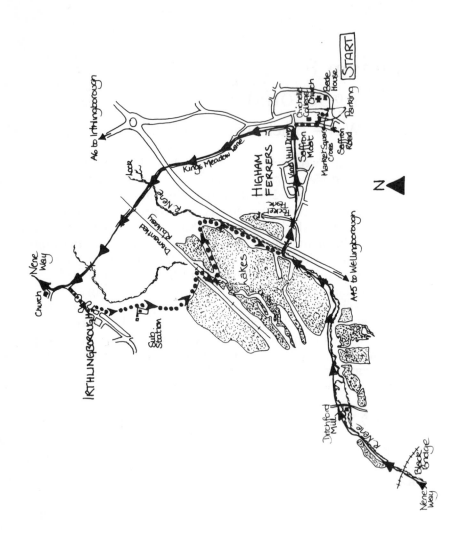

Higham Ferrers and Irthlingborough

(Nene Way – Black Bridge to Irthlingborough)

Introduction: Two ancient towns are linked together by this stretch of the Nene Way. Higham Ferrers in particular has a rich heritage, reflected in its venerable church, Bede House and fine buildings in the conservation area. A walkabout centring on the Market Square is sure to enhance the day. There are intriguing little alleyways to be explored, twisting away from the wide street of this flourishing old town, dominated by the exquisite, soaring spire of St Mary's church.

This circular walk gives the opportunity to return to Higham Ferrers from Irthlingborough on lakeside paths, a magnet for anglers and birdwatchers alike. At the Riverside Pocket Park nature reserve, tended by local conservationists, there is a welcome seat to be found in the butterfly garden before arriving back at Higham Ferrers via Saffron Moat, where part of the medieval fishponds still survives.

Distance: Black Bridge to Irthlingborough on the Nene Way about 5.5 miles. Circular walk around 4 miles.

Refreshments: A range of pubs in both towns, most serving food, though none directly en route.

How to get there: Higham Ferrers is on the A6 between Kettering and Bedford, as is Irthlingborough. There is limited parking on the Market Square, also a larger car park in Saffron Road where the walk begins. OS Landranger series 1:50 000 maps 152 Northampton & Milton Keynes, 153 Bedford & Huntingdon.

Nene Way – Black Bridge to Irthlingborough: Follow the ninth section of the Nene Way from the railway viaduct at Black Bridge, to the ancient site of Ditchford Mill. Continue on along the perimeter of Anglian Water and the Skew Bridge Club, on the other side of the lakes. The Way then sweeps over the bridge across the A45 and up into Higham Ferrers to Saffron Road.

There is a public car park to the right where the circular walk begins, which gives easy access through an open gateway in an ancient wall to the Market Square, for an additional treat. Before leaving, look back over your shoulder to the mural painted on a factory wall, facing the park. Join the circular walk to Irthlingborough, then continue by turning to Walk Ten.

The Walk: From the Market Square car park, turn back into Saffron Road. The carved stone archway and iron gate (right) marks the enclosure of Chichelle College, and in the park opposite is Saffron Moat and a fragment of the fishponds which were dug for the fellows of the college.

Join the Nene Way on the corner of Saffron Road and Vine Hill Road. The marker post is across from the elaborate cemetery gate and points straight over, as far as the next curve. The road then changes to a rough track, Kings Meadow Lane, between double hedges to the A45.

Cross with care in a direct line to the bridge over the river Nene, which divides here for the lock. The next stretch, to the disused railway line, tends to be tricky in winter weather owing to muddy conditions.

Carry on across the flat bed of the valley to Irthlingborough, toward the gaunt tower of the church of St Peter. A combination of square and rounded architecture, from this angle it appears to be detached from the main body of the church. Join the lower end of St Peter's Way.

On the hill, the **Nene Way** carries on through the churchyard toward the A6. At the top of the road, just out of sight, stands the Market Cross on a circular island at the parting of the roads. The shops, pubs and toilets are in this vicinity, in the main part of town.

To continue on the circuit, almost opposite the church gate turn into Oak Terrace between bungalows and the stone walls and gateway of the secluded Louise Lilley Homes, to Spinney Terrace. Turn left in front of the factory.

Down the close now, where grey and terracotta brick paths weave through a modern estate to a lower level, bearing to the right. At the last new bungalow, the path departs from the road to follow a short roughly fenced pathway through the allotments. It then goes diagonally over a field and round the bottom side, passing the electricity sub-station with the slender spire of Higham Ferrers church on the far horizon.

At the hedgeline, turn left on the track beside large private fishing ponds, reclaimed from the former gravel pits. Zigzagging right, then left through the hedge and over the two bridges, noting the 'danger deep water' signs. Go over the hump between vigorous bushes and brambles growing over the dismantled railway line.

The path now runs along a raised strip of land dividing two more broad lakes, in a rather wild area, a magnet for birdwatchers and anglers alike. Turn right at the end, and walk beside the river parallel to the A45, to the span of the contemporary footbridge. Rejoin the Nene Way here.

Carry on over the lesser wooden bridge and kissing-gate at the bottom of the Wharf Road, as the path soon leaves to cross the Riverside Pocket Park nature reserve, where there is a restful seat in the butterfly garden, tended by the local conservation group.

Over the stile, a brief gloom descends as the light diminishes under the high hedges. The path rises to the cul-de-sac and crosses, to emerge at Vine Hill Drive, which in turn merges with Saffron Road to return to the town.

Historical Notes

Ditchford Mill (Nene Way): A mill was already on this spot in the 13th century, with a bridge crossing beside it. The old bridge is now suffering under the burden of heavy traffic for which it was not built, and needs constant repair. This used to be a lively place for camping, boating and swimming, when local folk would flock here on outings at the week-ends. Later, the Blisworth to Peterborough railway crossed here, but was axed, like many others, by Beeching. Now a commercial factory, Ditchford Mill has witnessed many changes over the centuries. These days only the rumble of cumbersome vehicles is heard as they travel back and forth to the industrial units and the creeping gravel workings.

Higham Ferrers: The name Higham Ferrers is derived from the Saxon 'hech ham' meaning 'a settlement on a hill'. A Norman castle was constructed here in the late 11th century by William Peverell who held the manor of Higham. After falling into disrepair, the stone was removed and sold to build Kimbolton Castle in 1523. The land passed to the prominent Ferrers family, in 1199, who gave their name to the town and were instrumental in gaining the first Borough Charter in 1520, which remained in force until 1974. Henry III's son, Edmund Crouchback, Earl of Lancaster, built a second castle, of which only a morsel of the mound now exists, to the north of the church. The estate then passed to the Crown and is still under the Duchy of Lancaster.

Behind the ancient Market Square, Cross and Town Hall, the fantastic spire of St Mary's rises and beckons the walker to stroll through the side alley, in this elegantly preserved conservation area. In the grounds of the church is the Bede House, built in layers of ironstone and limestone, originally intended to house twelve poor men and a housekeeper. With the Chantry Chapel, used as a grammar school until 1907 and the church itself, dating from the 13th century, they comprise a handsome trio of ecclesiastical treasures.

The founder of the grammar school, the Bede House and Chichelle College, was Henry Chichelle. Born in 1362, the son of a yeoman, he was educated at Oxford and Winchester and was to become Archbishop of Canterbury. He died in 1443 and was buried in Canterbury Cathedral.

Saffron Moat, now a public park, has retained a small part of the fishponds, though hardly recognisable to the casual passer-by. It is sometimes referred to as 'the cup and saucer pond', owing to its shape. The name Saffron is thought to have been taken from the cultivation of the saffron plant, used at that time for flavouring and dyes.

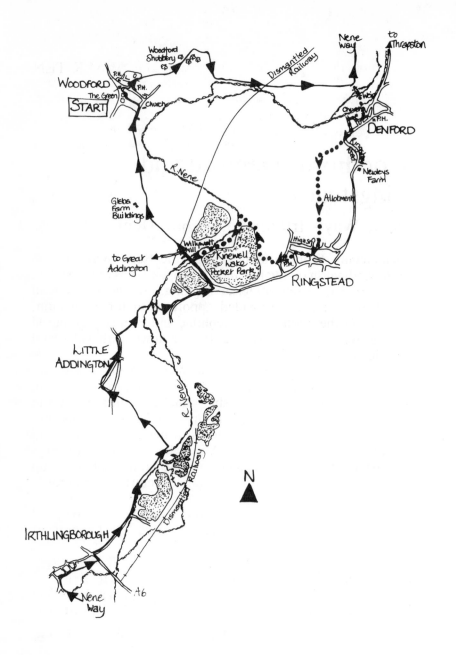

Woodford, Denford and Ringstead

(Nene Way – Irthlingborough to Denford)

Introduction: From Irthlingborough the Nene Way rises to Little Addington on the hill and gives open vistas of the valley, a rich area for archaeological exploration. The widespread gravel extraction has provided opportunities for excavation, resulting in the discovery of Neolithic and Bronze Age burial sites as well as evidence of a Roman town with villas and heating systems at Stanwick.

This circular walk joins the Nene Way at Woodford, where the church is said to be haunted, and follows it to Denford, in its riverside setting. The Aylesbury ducks are an attraction in their own right. The walk then returns via Ringstead – another ghostly tale! – and through peaceful Kinewell Lake park and nature reserve. At Willy Watt Mill, where the waterwheel is still now but there is a busy lock and marina, the walk picks up the route of the Nene Way once again to return to Woodford.

Distance: Irthlingborough to Woodford on the Nene Way 5.2 miles. Just over 5 miles on the circular walk. OS Landranger series 1:50 000 map 141 Kettering & Corby.

Refreshments: In Little Addington (Nene Way) The Bell public house and restaurant are popular. The Duke's Arms and The White Horse are adjacent to the green in Woodford. The

Cock Inn is over the river at Denford, in the High Street. The Axe and Compass is on the walk in Ringstead.

How to get there: Woodford is 1 mile south of the A604 Kettering to Thrapston road, but there is no access from the A1/M1 link road (A14). The walk begins by the green.

Nene Way – Irthlingborough to Denford: The tenth section of the Nene Way continues through St Peter's churchyard at Irthlingborough, with its old tombstones and typical heavy yews to Nene View, which as the name implies affords glimpses of the wide expanse of meadows. Beside Hall Farm, the path filters between walls of stone and brick behind terraced houses, and eventually reaches the Bedford road.

Cross dogleg over the A6 (ie left and then right) to the bridleway and walk on to the weir and the perimeter of the Frontier Camp activity area. Stay on the bank until the Way branches off to the left, leaving the river, on a long uphill diagonal trek to the rear of the industrial units at Little Addington.

Cross to Chapel Hill, and go around the bend to Parliament Row, St Mary's church, The Bell and Amen Place, leaving the village loop to meet the Great Addington road and turn to the left. In a short distance, the Nene Way slopes over a couple of fields and briefly joins the waterside. Here is the first of a chain of huge square stepping-stones, a relic of the days of severe flooding, and no doubt still useful in winter.

Go over a substantial bridge, lock and sluice gates to the disused railway line, which is in close proximity to the medieval site of Mallows Cotton (a medieval word meaning 'cottages'). Ringstead Grange trout fishery is on the corner just before the T junction for Ringstead, but turn left into Addington Road for the Willy Watt Mill and Woodford. Follow the Nene Way markers to Woodford village. Now follow the route of the circular walk as far as Denford, then continue by turning to Walk Eleven.

The Walk: Start at the green in Woodford, facing The Duke's Arms, and go downhill toward the White Horse inn. Turn left along Whittlesea Terrace to the Nene Way post set between blocks of houses, and go over the stile and rough pasture to the corner of the field.

Pass into The Shrubbery, once known as Stone Pit Common, by an iron gate and at the end of the woodland, turn at a right angle. You are looking over the A1/M1 link road (A14) and the former site of Islip Furnaces, long since demolished. Turn right again, to the stile and down to the river, staying on the nearside bank. After the handgate, cross the old railway line over the meadows to the siphonic weir, leaving the **Nene Way** which goes on to Islip.

Continue the walk by crossing the river and making your way into Denford village. Turn right, into the High Street, where there are several 17th century houses. Go down Church Lane, passing around or through the graveyard of the lovely church of the Holy Trinity, and left at the end, to the main road.

On leaving the village and turning right towards Ringstead, a fingerpost on the bend shows the way, initially with hedge to the right, then bearing left to run parallel with the Ringstead road and Newleys Farm on the hill.

The path continues close to the allotments at Ringstead and goes through to the High Street, heading for The Axe and Compass in Carlow Road. Across from the pub, turn into Meadow Close and go around the corner, where the path is next to a 'private road' sign, and leads to Kinewell Lake. Walking in a northerly direction, follow the shoreline about halfway round the Pocket Park, eventually coming close to the river Nene again at Willy Watt Mill (private fishing).

Out on the Ringstead/Addington road, pass over the bridge with its single cutwater, looking over the parapet at the disintegrating water-wheel, with a weir on the other side. It is usually lined with a string of moored boats. Go to the sharp corner ahead, now picking up the Nene Way again.

Follow the signs due north over the stiles, dismantled railway and hill, almost as far as Glebe Farm buildings, where the path branches off to the right and continues close to the river, crossing a concrete track. The outskirts of Woodford will be in sight, and the church behind the trees, then over the hump.

Pass The Rectory and the secluded De Capell House and go on up the hill at Church Green beside the beautiful stone walls, to exit via Pound Lane and back to the green.

Historical Notes

Willy Watt Mill has endured a multitude of changes since the early mill was first mentioned in the Domesday Book. It has been involved in the processing of cloth, in grinding corn, in paper making, the pulverising of bones for fertilisers, then back to flour milling. The water-wheels are stilled, for now only the lock and marina are busy, and peace has returned.

Woodford: The church of St Mary the Virgin was a scene of controversy in recent years, when two boys interested in photography and old churches produced a transparency showing a figure in white kneeling before the altar. The phantom was never seen again, nor reliably identified, but some thought it might have been Sir Walter Traillys, who was lord of the manor 700 years ago. His heart is wrapped in a cloth and rests within a pillar in the north side of the nave. Other possibilities have been suggested, such as the Reverend Basil Everley Owen, an admired rector of the parish, who passed away in 1963, or perhaps it was the ghost of Roger de Kineton, who died in 1280.

Industry here was in ironstone mining, limestone pits and furnaces. Manure from the working horses was astutely put to commercial use in growing mushrooms which were then sold to Covent Garden. A cobbler, blacksmith and undertaker, and later a clothing factory with its own female football team, were sources of employment for the villagers, but such trades melted away as people travelled further field.

Denford: The gaggle of Aylesbury ducks is a constant attraction at Denford, where they are always on the move on and around the river banks. Even the road sign forewarns the driver 'ducks and children crossing!'

The village at one time had a school for youngsters of all ages, but when it closed in the 1950s the children walked across the fields to Ringstead in summer and had to walk by road in winter or hope for a ride, if they were lucky. An early walker par excellence was Josiah Eaton of this parish, who walked 51 miles from London to Colchester, returning the next day to repeat the journey for 20 consecutive days!

Fortunate home-owners have gardens sweeping down to the river, with superb willows and private berthing. Coal and corn barges came this way, to and fro from Thrapston, and one of the old warehouses and loading platforms has been cleverly converted to a delightful waterside shangri-la.

Ringstead: Ringstead also has its very own ghost in the form of Lydia Ailey, a single pregnant lady of some notoriety living in the 1800s. Her married lover was charged with her murder, although at the time there was no body and he was released by the magistrates. However, some years later a female body was found and he was re-arrested, only to be freed when several other corpses came to light on the old site of an itinerants' burial ground. In 1906 yet another skeleton was discovered in a farmer's field, and a doctor from Thrapston verified certain details, but the coroner decided against a further enquiry. Now Lydia's ghost is said to haunt Meeting Lane!

Peaceful Kinewell Park, recovered from gravel workings, has taken on a new role as a Pocket Park and wildlife refuge, covering 47 acres. It is leased to the parish council by the extraction company at a cost of £1 per annum, for 99 years.

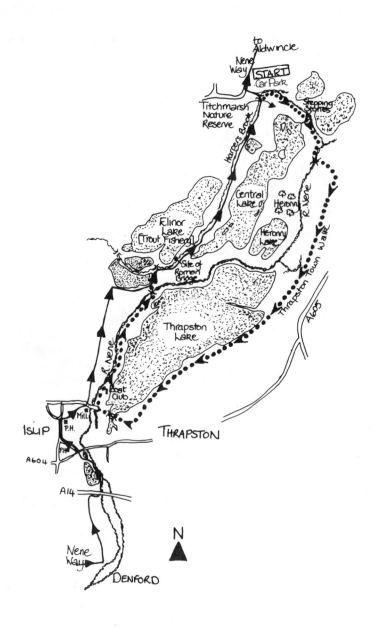

to Aldwincle

Nene
Way

START
Car Park

Stepping
Stones

Titchmarsh
Nature
Reserve

Harpers Brook

Central
Lake

Heronry

R. Nene

Elinor
Lake
(Trout Fishery)

Heronry
Lake

Site of
Roman
Bridge

Thrapston Town Wall

A605

R. Nene

Thrapston
Lake

Boat
Club

ISLIP

Mill

P.H.

P.H.

THRAPSTON

A604

A14

Nene
Way

DENFORD

N

Titchmarsh Nature Reserve and Thrapston Lake

(Nene Way – Denford to Aldwincle)

Introduction: The Nene Way wends on from Denford to the delights of the Nature Reserve, which is where this beautiful circular walk begins. This really is a birdwatcher's paradise. Binoculars are a good idea, to make the most of the heronry, lakes and landscaped islands which unfold before you. There is a constant sense of tranquillity and you are never far from the water as you make your way past Thrapston Lake to Islip. Here the return route picks up the Nene Way near Islip Mill, where eels were trapped for the London market in the 19th century. Through water meadows and by lakes and a deep-flowing brook, the walk returns to the delights of the Reserve.

Distance: Reserve walk less than 5 miles. Nene Way section 4.3 miles. OS Landranger series 1:50 000 map 141 Kettering & Corby.

Refreshments: At Islip only. There is the Woolpack Inn and Motel and adjoining Golden Fleece Tea-rooms, and also The Rose and Crown.

How to get there: Visitors to the Reserve are requested to use the car park on the Lowick Road at Aldwincle, from which the circular walk is described. Aldwincle can be reached from either the east of the A6116 Corby bypass or to the west of the A605.

Nene Way – Denford to Aldwincle: The Nene Way goes on from Denford, barely brushing the village and not crossing the main river. It edges past the siphonic weir, which is a device to control the flow of minor streams into the main river, so as to maintain the level of water for navigation, bringing another feature of interest to the walker along the journey. Go over the disused railway line and A14 to meet the A604 at Thrapston Bridge in Islip. In the medieval era, a toll was levied, but allowed soldiers and churchgoers to pass without payment. The nine arch bridge of today (five arches of which were destroyed by torrential flood in 1795) has been massively modified since medieval times and is the result of increasing pressure on the roads over the centuries.

Cross over to The Woolpack Inn (Rockingham Forest Tourist Information) and follow the discs around the bend to High Street, passing Islip House set back from the path, to The Rose and Crown at the corner of Mill Lane.

Sharp right here through the pub yard, keeping to the left and over two fields to a stile just above Islip Mill. Now a private residence, eels used to be trapped here and sold in London in the late 1800s. Cross the lane and continue in the meadow along the river on the left bank to a scrubby spinney and go slightly right around the edge. From the bridge, the Way keeps to the deep channel of Harper's Brook and then curves between Central and Elinor Lakes, the latter being a trout fishery, and close to the discovery of the footings of a Roman bridge.

The hide, sponsored by Oundle School, is in memory of Sir Peter Scott, who frequently came to watch the waders here when a pupil at the school. It is conveniently set next to the wader scrape, and so provides an excellent observation post.

Leave the area of the Titchmarsh Nature Reserve by the notice board, and continue on the Nene Way towards Aldwincle. Turn to Walk Twelve.

The Walk: The notice board at the start of the circuit is close to the car park in Titchmarsh Nature Reserve. Do pause to read this notice, designed to acquaint the walker with details of the Reserve, and abide by the plea to keep to marked footpaths and keep dogs under control at all times.

Follow the trail marked 'to Titchmarsh' along the northern boundary of Brancey Brook, a branch of the Nene, to the row of circular concrete stepping-stones which span the overflow from the lake. (This section is not to be recommended to the faint-hearted or unattended children and may be unsuitable to cross after heavy rain or flood.)

Continue to observe the waymarks, past the hide on the peninsula, donated by a private individual and the Northants Bird Club. To the left is the mill and boat moorings, and in front the distant church at Titchmarsh.

Leaving the Reserve, be prepared for the ford flowing across the lane, but with a sturdy railed bridge for the walker, and walk up the track to the beginning of the dismantled railway line, now transformed to the Thrapston Town Walk.

Tantalising views of the heronry, lakes and landscaped islands make the use of binoculars worthwhile, to enjoy the nesting sites of some of the birds and the muddy shores exposed for migrating waders.

The path narrows in places, flanked by pretty copses and the occasional seat, never far from the edge of the water. Although the A605 runs parallel, on the crest of the hill, there remains here a sense of tranquillity. Across Thrapston Lake, the private boat club is situated on the far bank and the outskirts of the town are to the left.

On reaching the lane near the playing fields at Chancery

89

Lane, bear to the right, through the anglers' car park, past the boat slipway and over the iron bridge. The exit to the mill and lane to Islip is over the second bridge.

Prior to that bridge, walk along the track, now between lake and river, backed by water-meadows where large flocks of Canada geese gather to roam noisily in the colder weather. Over one more bridge and stile, the path joins the Nene Way again. Follow the Way back to the Reserve car park, between the lakes and along Harpers Brook.

Historical Notes

Thrapston: King John granted a charter for a weekly market for Thrapston (a pre-Christian name), which is still acknowledged to be of prime importance in this region. Best known for its livestock auctions, the regular cattle sales have earned a fine reputation for consistent quality.

Islip: Several refurbished homes mingle with older dwellings with thatched roofs, some built of limestone, which is indigenous to this county.

When horsepower was the driving force in agriculture and trade, the making of horse-collars was of essential concern. Rushes were harvested from the river and the work carried out in a factory, now converted to the working men's club.

The Titchmarsh Nature Reserve: The 150 acre spread of the Reserve consists of a large collection of lakes and islands, resulting from former gravel extractions begun here in 1926; a recurring phenomenon along this valley.

The Northants County Council, the Nature Conservancy Council and Countryside Commission grants, a generous gift from Barclaycard, Trust members working to raise funds and the assistance of the World Wildlife Fund, all enabled the Trust to purchase this prime property.

In winter, huge numbers of wildfowl, such as goosander, wigeon, teal, pochard, tufted duck and cormorants may be seen, along with ubiquitous coots and ducks. The distinctive Canada and greylag geese are present throughout the year. Migrating waders in evidence might be redshank, common sandpiper, greenshank and bar-tailed godwit, although some stay only briefly to feed on the muddy shores. Breeding here is favoured by the little and ringed plover on the shingle, and the unmistakable black and white oystercatcher.

The heronry, now a SSSI (Site of Special Scientific Interest), originally created in 1885 by Lord Lilford, is set aside in a more remote sector and is a sensitive area closed to the public for obvious reasons. The birds nest in the tall trees, early in the year, with their young appearing around the month of May. These large birds are easily recognisable by their grey, black and white plumage, the neck withdrawn in flight. They display a slow wing-beat, with wings held in an arched position, pointing downwards at the tips, and feed on a diet of frogs, voles, fish and eels, of which there is a bountiful supply.

Recolonised plants now cover the bare patches of ground and attract hordes of insects, as the innumerable species of butterflies and dragonflies are drawn to their various food sources and breeding choices. Wildflowers grow in profusion and the grassland is dotted with great burnet (rose family), delicate cowslips (primrose family), white sneezewort (daisy family) and the red bartsia (figwort family). Damp swathes support purple loosestrife, marsh dock, speedwell and other less familiar plants.

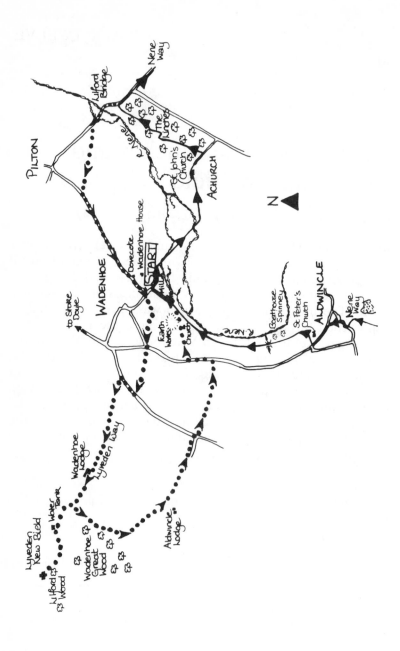

Wadenhoe, The Linches and Lyveden New Bield

(Nene Way – Aldwincle to The Linches)

Introduction: This superb walking country offers two circular walks of singular delight. From Wadenhoe it is a gentle stroll over to Lyveden New Bield, built by Sir Thomas Tresham in the 17th century and now under the auspices of the National Trust. The intriguing edifice, which was never completed, is approached through Lilford Wood, where the elusive fallow deer roam. Returning through Wadenhoe Great Wood to the village, you can if you wish continue on the second short walk, in the opposite direction and through an entirely different landscape. This walk picks up the route of the Nene Way, crossing the water meadows to the gracious church of St John the Baptist at Thorpe Achurch and the wooded scarp of the river, The Linches, to the enchanting Lilford bridge, before winding back to Wadenhoe once more.

Distance: Circular walk 'A' excluding Lyveden New Bield 3 miles, and Walk 'B' 2.5 miles. Nene Way section 3 miles. OS Landranger series 1:50 000 map 141 Kettering and Corby.

Refreshments: The Kings Head is on the riverside at Wadenhoe, and teas are available at the village hall on Sundays only.

How to get there: Wadenhoe is to the west of the A605, turning off at Thorpe Waterville midway (4 miles) between Thrapston and Oundle. The walk starts at Mill Lane.

Nene Way – Aldwincle to The Linches: Entering Aldwincle from the Lowick road, this twelfth section of the Nene Way cuts through to the main street (Pear Tree Farm to the right) to St Peter's church (to left). Go over the stiles between The Rectory and a modest cluster of stone houses, to a third stile.

Turn sharp left here and stick to the headland of two fields, with a hedge to the left then changing to hedge to the right. There are glorious views over undulating rural tranquillity, with the church spire of Achurch peeking through the trees. Drifting downhill, a few giant sequoias (redwoods) tower above their neighbours in Boathouse Spinney, before the Way crosses double stiles separated by a bridge, prior to reaching a SSSI on a stretch of diverse wetland.

The woodland here has been known, since the 15th century, as Conygher (indicating a rabbit warren). It gives tantalising glimpses of the river, before coming to a tranquil glade of lofty ash trees, with a timely resting place in the shape of a felled tree. Cross the trickling springs on hefty sleepers to the next field.

The church of St Michael and All Angels at Wadenhoe stands proud on a high hill of old grassland, with a seat set on the path, overlooking the beautiful scenery. Sounds of water herald the weir and lock. The village hall and The King's Head, built of local limestone, with oak beams and stone flags inside, are through the weighted gate. Caroline Cottage, partway up Church Street, was originally the village school.

The quaint gatehouse with the circular window and bright front door is facing, as you turn right into Mill Lane. You now join the route of the circular walk to The Linches. When the Nene Way continues on, turn for the next section to Walk Thirteen.

The Walk: Start the walk to The Linches (**Walk A**) by joining the Nene Way at Mill Lane in Wadenhoe village. The lane winds down next to ivy-clad walls overhung by wondrous sycamore and ash trees, wrapping around Wadenhoe House.

The sound of the millrace in the background increases at Mill House, as the path goes under the chestnuts and past the stables to the white bridge over the ford, where carts and animals used to cross to the pastures.

Follow the Nene Way over the flat water-meadows and the high angular bridge, to the stile in the corner. Take a diagonal line past the spreading chestnut trees to the stile at the lower end of the graveyard of St John the Baptist in Achurch. The church was built around 1300, with a stunning tower and broach spire. Take a moment to look at the carved oak memorial lychgate and the walls and barns of the Old Rectory, hidden among the foliage.

In the lane, follow the Nene Way sign as it branches off into The Linches, opposite a mysterious derelict house. This is a private woodland, managed by the Forestry Commission, where walkers are requested to keep strictly to the riding and path (and dogs on leads please). It turns down the steps to run along the escarpment parallel with the gurgling water, to the Lilford-Pilton road. Here the **Nene Way** continues to the right.

Leave the Nene Way and turn downhill, where the fence borders Lilford Park, to the most handsome stone bridge, revealing an exquisite cameo of the lock and secluded river banks.

Cross the smaller bridge and very shortly a fingerpost points over the fields, at a slanting angle. The path eventually joins the Pilton-Wadenhoe road, and the rooftops of the hamlet of Achurch peep from the dense trees over the valley. Turn left towards Wadenhoe and on entering the village, note North Lodge and the intriguing entrance to Wadenhoe House. After the bend, in the paddock, stands the circular limestone dovecote, topped by a Collyweston slate roof. At the road junction, turning left will bring you back to Mill Lane, but if you want to continue on the second walk to Lyveden New Bield, turn right.

Walk B starts at the double gate opposite the Postal Telegraph Office in the main street, set back next to the delightful Bearshank House, which was fashioned from stone from a former barn in nearby Bearshank Wood.

The path bears to the right and over a stile into a dish-shaped meadow, up a bosky bank next to huge rock slabs. Joining the Lyveden Way, it goes toward a sign at the junction of the Wadenhoe-Aldwincle road. Cross straight over the next field to the drift road (green lane), where the fingerpost is in sight on the right, to go through the gate on the bridleway to Wadenhoe Lodge.

Just after the outlying grey stone lodge, a waymark shows the path between lanky hedges into the dip, which may be somewhat rough after the passage of horses. It comes out on a track.

To continue to Lyveden New Bield only, 1 mile away, walk up the hill parallel with the trees as far as the raised water tank, almost surrounded by woodland and devoid of habitation. Veer away over the field toward tree stumps and the little bridge in the hollow, to enter Lilford Wood on the riding. Exit with Lyveden New Bield directly in front. There is a longer return route waymarked via Lady Wood if desired.

Otherwise, with no diversion, bear left on the track and just on the curve (before buildings) branch off to the right on a broad grass margin, keeping to the fenceline to the stout meshed gate in the corner. Pass through to take a diagonal line toward a clump of trees, behind which lies Aldwincle Lodge.

A few yards in from the corner, go through a gap in the hedge past a ring of hawthorns and in the second field, stay to the right of the shallow pond to the handgate in the far corner. (On no account use the private approach to the residence.)

Cross the green lane again to the opposite unfenced field,

keeping to the right of the hedgeline, with the landscape falling away to the lush Nene Valley. On reaching the Wadenhoe-Aldwincle road, a short stretch of road walking (left) soon opens to Church Field and the Northamptonshire Scout Council official camp site. Take care over the cattle-grid and make for the ancient church of St Michael and All Angels, which graces the rise, with extensive earthworks to one side.

The village is nestled behind the hill and the beauty of the dwellings is unveiled on descending the mound to The King's Head and the pleasant riverside gardens.

Historical Notes

Aldwincle (Nene Way): Aldwincle was formerly split into two parishes, each with its own medieval church and parish priest. St Peter's has an elegant broach spire, and All Saints, at the far end of the village, still stands in splendour. Dating from the 13th century, it fell into disuse but remains well tended.

John Dryden, born in 1631 at the former rectory, now Dryden House, was to become a writer, poet, satirist and playwright, and Poet Laureate to Charles II. He died in May 1706 and was buried in Westminster Abbey.

Wadenhoe: The old Saxon words for ford 'waden', and 'hoe' a hill, were combined to create this descriptive name of Wadenhoe, on the north bank of the river Nene.

Granted by Edward VI in 1551 to Sir Walter Mildmay, the manor came into the keeping of the Hunt family, whose heirs were killed in Italy. The estate passed to the Right Hon George Ward-Hunt, who held the high office of Chancellor of the Exchequer in Disraeli's Cabinet in 1868 and was responsible for adding one penny to the income tax to subsidise the Abyssinian War. He was also the First Lord of the Admiralty and consequently, the village has the first Postal Telegraph Office in England, in order that he might be kept informed of government business. The village was also to the fore in having a gasworks to provide street lighting, established in 1869, on the site now occupied by the new village hall.

Wadenhoe House dates from 1657 and stands within its own park surrounded by massive trees and a mellowed stone wall. The fine dovecote has the original ladder and pole (potence) used to collect the birds' eggs, which were a valuable source of protein in the old days, from 500 plaster and lath nesting boxes.

The Mill House is in an idyllic setting, where a mill has existed since first recorded in the Domesday Book.

The church of St Michael and All Angels stands over the medieval earthworks and is a must for those who appreciate fine English churches. The Norman saddleback tower is one of the very few in the county, and the church bears traces of Saxon origin. The arches are from the 13th and 14th centuries, likewise the clerestory.

The memorials inside, down the stone steps, date from 1629. One poignant tablet is to the memory of Thomas and Caroline Welch-Hunt, who lost their lives to bandits whilst travelling on their honeymoon in Italy in 1824. Another is to the local schoolmistress, whose benevolence enabled four windows to be dedicated to her memory. Other stained glass and plate remembers Sir Michael Culme-Seymour and his wife, late of Rockingham Castle, who lived at Wadenhoe House for some years. The Royal Arms and shield, in the ringing chamber, are worthy of special note, as are the handsome altar frontal, pulpit fall and offertory bags, enhanced by the gold braid from the fine robes of the late Chancellor Ward-Hunt.

Lyveden New Bield: Built by Sir Thomas Tresham, a devoted Catholic, Lyveden New Bield symbolises the Passion of Christ and religious themes, in the form of a Greek cross. Being a wealthy man, most of the materials such as stone and timber came from his own vast estates, where he was also heavily involved (at Rothwell and Rushton) with similar projects. The work was not completed at the death of Sir Thomas in 1605, but is thought to have been continued by his son, Sir Lewis. However, the shell of the four-winged house may be seen today, as then, roofless and remote, accessible only by an uphill track. It is open to the public.

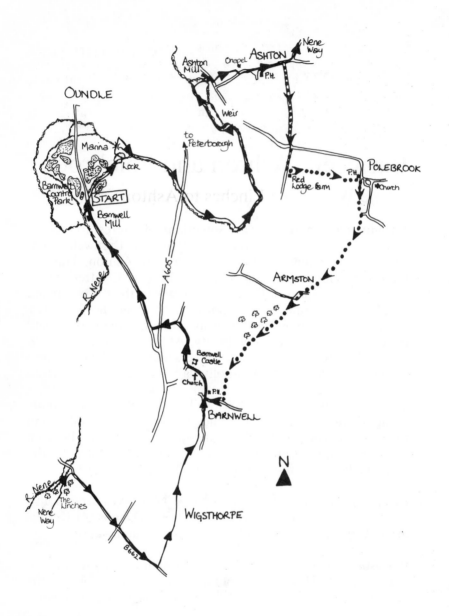

OUNDLE

Marina

Lock

Barnwell
Country
Park

START

Barnwell
Mill

R. Nene

A605

Ashton
Mill

Chapel   ASHTON

Nene
Way

P.H.

Weir

to Peterborough

POLEBROOK

Red
Lodge Farm

P.H.

Church

ARMSTON

Barnwell
Castle

Church

P.H.

BARNWELL

N

R. Nene

The
Linches

Nene
Way

WIGSTHORPE

B662

Barnwell, Ashton and Polebrook
(Nene Way – The Linches to Ashton)

Introduction: There is always something of interest to be seen as this circular walk joins the Nene Way near Barnwell Country Park and meanders along by the river to Ashton. Tranquil reed beds, smooth flowing water and aged willow trees make this a lasting pleasure. Even the stiles, with their broad plank treads, must be rated as some of the best along the Way! The village of Ashton is tucked away from the main road and refreshingly retains its individuality. At Polebrook, as the walk begins the circuit back, winter walkers may be lucky enough to see circus animals such as woolly llamas enjoying a rest from their summertime travels. Through the little hamlet of Armston, the walk heads for Barnwell. Barnwell Manor, family home of HRH the Duke of Gloucester, is the only royal seat in the county. The spectacular ruins of the castle may be seen from the Nene Way, which takes the walker back to the Country Park where this walk started.

Distance: Circular walk about 8 miles. Nene Way section also about 8 miles. OS Landranger series 1:50 000 maps 141 Kettering & Corby, 142 Peterborough and surrounding area.

Refreshments: Barnwell Mill and restaurant is on the old Oundle road. There is an abundant choice of establishments nearby in Oundle. Ashton Mill Tea-Rooms are open on summer Sundays only, and The Chequered Skipper is on the green. In Polebrook, there is The King's Arms and in Barnwell, The Montagu Arms, which also offers accommodation and has a caravan site.

How to get there: The circular walk starts at Barnwell Country Park, where there are ample parking facilities, picnic areas and toilets. It is only about a hundred yards or so from the field entrance to the river at the marina. The park is adjacent to Barnwell Mill, where the Nene Way crosses the road to start the circuit. The Park can be reached to the west of the A605 Peterborough road.

Nene Way – The Linches to Ashton: Continue on this thirteenth section by walking up the steep hill from The Linches, to the twin gatehouses at the entrance to Lilford Hall and straight over the A605, another Roman road. It is about 1 mile in all, on the B662, to the old railway bridge. Follow the sign left, on a narrow track, passing the stone built Hall Farm, to the minuscule hamlet of Wigsthorpe. On to Barnwell, go to the left of Wigsthorpe Farm Cottage and over the fields. Then staying beside the brook, pass the lonely chancel of All Saints' church, to The Montagu Arms at the crossroads. (The circular walk returns to this point.)

Continue beside the stream, passing houses of charm and character, to the enchanting little bridge, purpose built for the former Duke of Gloucester to walk through to St Andrew's church. The grand ruins of Barnwell Castle sit solidly on the hill, as the path runs beneath the surrounding walls.

At the T junction, turn to the right around the bend, to a Nene Way post on the left side pointing down and quickly up at Empty Spinney. Cross the Oundle bypass to a short byway, linking to the old Oundle road.

Carry on past the garden centre to Barnwell Mill and almost opposite, the Way enters a field. A brass plaque commemorates the opening of the Irchester to Wansford section of the Nene Way by HRH the Duke of Gloucester, on 25th April 1990. Here you join the route of the circular walk as far as Ashton – continue with Walk Fifteen.

The Walk: Join the Nene Way where it enters a field opposite Barnwell Mill. The path runs between the lakes and the river Nene, backed by the marina basin. Proceed over the lock and two bridges, hugging the bank as the gentle river weaves through undisturbed pastures, with aged fallen willows lying at obscure angles over the rustling reed-beds.

Go under the bypass, built on the line of the disused railway, to a first class three-tread stile. Then you come to the placid tree-lined loop, where the branches sway with every breath of wind. The occasional fishermen melt into the thick waterside foliage. In this huge twist of the river, where the waterlily pads float dreamily, there is a private mooring and a brief glance of the needlelike spire of the church at Oundle.

Skirt the weir, lock and lacy willows, to the green bridge. Cross the high pipe bridge to the considerable reed-beds and Ashton Mill Museum and Tea-rooms, taking a peep over the wall to the pond.

Cross the road and up the steps, winding over to Ashton green and The Chequered Skipper, as the scenery now changes completely. Go on by the side of the pub, now passing a row of thatched estate cottages and a long, dark wooden barn, also thatched. At the left turn, the **Nene Way** carries on to Warmington.

Just prior to that, for the circular walk, the byway on the right runs down, partway beside a ditch, to meet the road to Polebrook. Cross in a straight line, and at the gate before Red Lodge Farm, go through three gates and stiles toward the village. Look out for the possibility of unusual circus animals, such as woolly llamas and ponies, spending time in their winter quarters.

A short sleeper bridge next as the pathway curves around a red-tiled house to exit at Keepers Cottage. To the left is The King's Arms and Polebrook village walk.

Turn right, without the diversion, to a path, where more animals may be encountered in a rough field, before joining another byway. The fingerpost shows the way across an unfenced roadside field, over a slatted bridge, to Armston.

Follow the lane only very briefly to another post pointing to Barnwell, skimming Armston Grove woodland. Walk down to meet the road with The Montagu Arms on the corner, rejoining the Nene Way in this beautiful setting. Follow the Nene Way back to Barnwell Country Park.

Historical Notes

Polebrook: The parish of Polebrook includes the outlying hamlets of Kingsthorpe and Armston, and has at its hub the curious church of All Saints. Rather strange in form, and basically dating from 1175–1250 with many additions in the subsequent centuries, the tower has a broach spire with three tiers of windows, set at an odd angle in relation to the body of the church, with simple benches inside, thought to be Jacobean. Founder member of the Royal Society (under the auspices of Charles II in 1662), Dr John Wilkins was brother-in-law to Oliver Cromwell and honoured rector of this church.

The memorials are in respect of members of the Ferguson family, who were resident at Polebrook Hall for 50 years. There is also a Roll of Honour to American servicemen killed in the Second World War. The 351st Bombardment Group operated from the nearby airfield, where a further memorial has been erected.

The first old age pensions were issued at the former post office, which moved premises more than once before fading away altogether, much to the chagrin of the villagers.

Polebrook Hall stems from the Jacobean period and has been extensively restored.

Barnwell: Barnwell Castle was built by Berngar de Moyne as a military fortress in about 1266, with circular bastions at each corner. The gatehouse is flanked by round towers, the whole encircled by a large courtyard, almost rectangular in shape, and surrounded by a moat. The living quarters were ranged around the bailey (outer defence wall) and have fireplaces and garderobes (wardrobes) for the lords and their retinues.

The castle passed to Peterborough Abbey in 1276, and after the Dissolution was bought by Sir Edward Montagu, who built a house in the courtyard. By 1540 the fortress was in reduced circumstances, and although partially restored by the Montagu family in 1586, it gradually fell into decline. The massive walls and towers make an impressive sight, retaining traces of habitation, but the moat has long since disappeared. Barnwell Manor grounds are open to the public twice a year, in the springtime (see National Gardens Scheme leaflet for details).

Only the chancel of All Saints' remains, at the lower end of the street, as the rest was razed in 1825. Precious memorials to the Montagu generations have been left undisturbed in their quiet resting place.

St Andrew's church in the middle of the village, dating from the 13th century, has a monument to the Reverend Nicholas Latham. He founded the almshouses in 1601, where the stone above the gateway is inscribed 'cast thy bread upon the water', as well as the first school.

A tollhouse and gate was originally situated at Barnwell Mill on the turnpike, following the Act of 1753. Wealthy trustees financed the scheme in order to thwart those travellers who had taken lesser roads to avoid the charges.

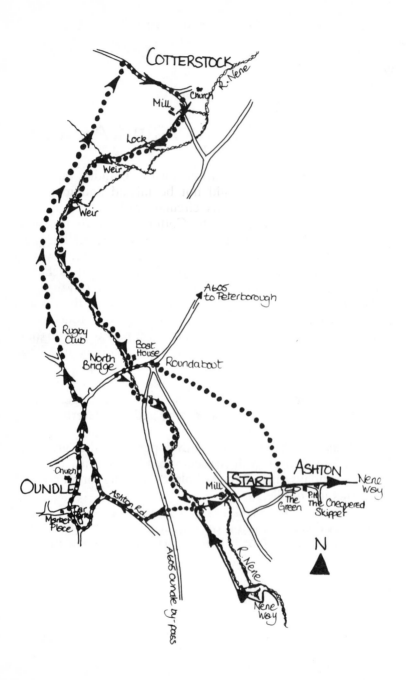

Oundle, Cotterstock and Ashton

Introduction: The ancient market town of Oundle, built on a spur above the river, should not be missed and makes an excellent focal point for this circular walk. Through open countryside the walk comes to Cotterstock, with its single village street, ancient church and medieval cross. Then the return route takes the walker along the river Nene, always a pleasure. When you reach the lovely symmetrical arches of North Bridge, you can either follow the river onwards, or make a detour to Ashton village, where every year the Conker Championships are held on the green. This walk touches the Nene Way only briefly, and does not form part of the ongoing route, but it can easily be picked up from the Way at Ashton Mill.

Distance: Approximately 5 miles. OS Landranger series 1:50 000 maps 141 Kettering & Corby and 142 Peterborough.

Refreshments: The Chequered Skipper, on the green at Ashton, and Ashton Mill Museum and Tea-rooms, open on summer Sundays only. Range of places catering for all pockets and tastes in Oundle.

How to get there: Ashton is off the A605 bypass at the roundabout at the end of North Bridge in Oundle, signed to Polebrook.

The Walk: Start between Ashton Mill and the pond, retracing the Nene Way for a few yards, to the green bridge. Go straight over the bypass, on a short posted path to Ashton Road. Turn right and carry on to the fork. Now there are two options.

A left turn, then right, will bring you to the car park and toilets via St Osyth's Place to the Market Square in Oundle, for those wishing to linger a while in this fine conservation area. The tapering medieval spire of St Peter's church soars dramatically from behind the buildings. After a perambulation, the walker can saunter down North Street to join the circuit at the football field.

Or, along to the right from the fork, the path carries on to the same football field, at the traffic lights on the main road to Peterborough.

Use the pavement, under the trees, as far as the garage and cross to New Road (before Riverside Maltings). In St Peter's Road, on the bend, take the unmade side turning to Occupation Road, which gives access to the tennis, rugby and bowls clubs. Go around the edge of the sports field and head for the riverside spinney bordering the sloping pasture. Go over the stile in the far corner. Continue topside of the trees, above the river, where the path eventually narrows between back gardens, to join the single village street of Cotterstock.

Turn right, with Cotterstock Hall over the road amid the trees, and the Old Vicarage dating from the 17th century. The medieval cross stands where the road divides for the ancient church, at Cotterstock House with its pretty cast iron veranda. Take the right fork to the mill, now put to commercial use after a disastrous fire which destroyed much of the original building.

At the gushing water of the sluice, a fingerpost indicates the riverside walk which goes over the weir. Enjoy the 'sounds of silence' and the subtle hues of the leaning willows hanging over the water. You will perhaps find empty shells along the field edges, picked clean by the waterbirds.

Keep following the river and after a couple more stiles and a bridge, the path approaches a group of wooden sheds, some thatched, forming the boat club. Branch off a little to the left to come up the embankment on to North Bridge, with its lovely symmetrical arches.

You can now continue on the slightly shorter lower walk back to Ashton Mill by crossing to the other side and down to the meadows. Follow the river onwards.

To extend the round to take in Ashton village, turn left toward the old railway station, now an industrial concern, and the neglected public house on the corner. Cross to the round-about and island, and over again to the stile and fingerpost, where the path stays next to the hedge for two fields. In the third it is edged on both sides by woodland, where one might be treated to the glorious display of a wandering peacock.

The path comes back to cross the front of the austere chapel, through the gate to the green at Ashton. Turn right, temporarily joining the Nene Way again (reverse direction), along the lane through the kissing-gate, down to Ashton Mill.

Historical Notes

Oundle: The market bell is still rung by tradition at midday on Thursday, to signify the right to the public market, which is indeed a busy thoroughfare, with all the stalls crammed together in the narrow Market Place. The Tudor-style cruciform Town Hall of 1826, has been agreeably converted to business premises and also houses the Tourist Information Centre. There are fine examples of Georgian housefronts and arched doorways, and quaint alleyways lead the eye and encourage the walker to investigate. St Peter's church has a most superb steeple and recessed spire, culminating in a tour de force of the English decorated style. Clearly visible from the street is the date inscribed 1634. There are many 13th century features within the church and without, to absorb the casual visitor.

A little further along the street, The Talbot Hotel of 1626, formerly known as The Tabrot (a tabard worn by heralds), occupies a prominent position and is a favoured rendezvous for all ages. Built of stone from Fotheringhay Castle, legend has it that the dark Jacobean staircase was the one trod by Mary Queen of Scots on the way to her execution, and bears the imprint of her ring. The panelling above and the window over-looking the turn of the stairs is purported to have been the one from which she took her final look in life, although many say neither is true. Founded in 1556, as a Free Grammar School, by the will of Sir William Laxton, a native of the town, grocer and Lord Mayor of London, the public school has many claims to fame. Many notable men received their education within these hallowed walls, including Sir Peter Scott, who was bestowed with a knighthood for his dedication to conservation. Several houses and cloisters comprise the present establishment.

In North Street, the National River Authority is now ensconced in the Old Rectory, behind high walls.

Several 18th and 19th century houses edging the street belong to Oundle School and Latham's Hospital, founded in 1611.

An inscription on the parapet of North Bridge records the destruction of the old bridge by flooding in 1570 and the ensuing rebuilding, and further work carried out between 1912–1914.

Ashton: Ashton, small though it may be with its manor house and cottages in Tudor style of thatch and local stone, was well ahead of its time when built around 1900 by Lord Rothschild. Bathrooms were fitted, where systems were serviced by water pumped from the river. Electricity was also introduced, generated from the same source at the mill, which had previously only been used for the grinding of corn. The cables were buried underground, so that the dwellings face the green in a charming setting devoid of ugly overhead lines.

The Chequered Skipper public house is named after an extinct butterfly, prolific until the 1960s but which then mysteriously disappeared. There are plans afoot, however, to reintroduce this colourful insect.

The green becomes the focus of attraction every autumn, when visitors flock here beneath the chestnut trees to witness the world annual Conker Championship.

Ashton Mill and Museum, only open at limited times, displays in situ turbines and engines from the Victorian era, local bygones and items relating to nature and conservation.

Excavations took place at Ashton prior to the construction of the Oundle bypass in the early 1980s, following a trial investigation ten years earlier. The fieldwork was to continue for several years and produced a large quantity of finds. Prehistoric remains, Iron Age traces and an unwalled Roman town and cemetery, yielded artefacts which are now in Peterborough Museum.

Cotterstock: Cotterstock is mentioned in the Domesday Book, and the name is thought to be derived from 'copper-stoc' meaning 'the place where the group gathered'.

One of the two manors here was established in connection with the medieval chantry college of priests, founded by John Gifford in 1338. He was a former rector, later to become royal clerk to Queen Isabella and thereafter, to Edward III. The manor was granted to the college by the queen, and consisted of two mills, meadows, a fishery and 85 acres of Rockingham Forest.

A second manor, from the Middle Ages, called Holts, passed to the Norton family. John Norton, a landowner and Parliamentarian during the Commonwealth, built the present Cotterstock Hall in 1656–58. The Hall was also frequented, at a later date, by the poet Dryden, when visiting his cousin, Elizabeth Steward.

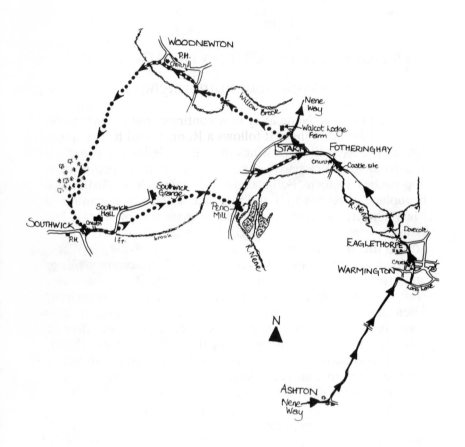

Fotheringhay and Woodnewton

(Nene Way – Ashton to Fotheringhay)

Introduction: The Nene Way now continues out of Ashton on its way to Fotheringhay. It follows a Roman road to Warmington and passes through Eaglethorpe, a delightful group of superb stone houses with a nearby medieval dovecote, as it approaches historic Fotheringhay. Fotheringhay Castle, the birthplace of Richard III and prison and place of execution of Mary Queen of Scots, is now just a grim pile of stones, but visitors from all over the world still make their way here to absorb the atmosphere.

This fascinating circular walk begins in Fotheringhay village and crosses pleasant countryside to Woodnewton. There is a craft workshop here which makes an interesting diversion. Then the walk crosses the Willow Brook as it makes its way towards Southwick. You may be lucky enough to spot deer as you stroll on a bracken-lined path through mixed woodland, and you will be rewarded with a view of Southwick Hall, set in spacious grounds, as you continue on down leafy lanes. The walk then returns to Fotheringhay, passing Perio Mill on the river Nene.

Distance: 4.2 miles from Ashton to Fotheringhay. Round walk about 6 miles. OS Landranger series 1:50 000 map 141 Kettering & Corby.

Refreshments: The Falcon Inn at Fotheringhay. In Woodnew-

113

ton, the very comfortable White Swan offers food and drink and a warm welcome to walkers. The thatched Shuckburgh Arms at Southwick is in the main street.

How to get there: Fotheringhay is off the A605 Oundle to Peterborough road, turning west at the cafe and filling station.

Nene Way – Ashton to Fotheringhay: The fourteenth section of the Nene Way begins by turning left at the isolated lodge on the corner, from Ashton. The Nene Way passes through the area of the rifle range (warnings when in operation!) on the byway.

Cross the road to Lutton and on past Tansor Grange. Bear right on entering Warmington, then left into Long Lane, facing the splendid church of St Mary the Virgin. Zigzag by the graveyard wall into Church Lane, Hautboy Lane and round the bend to the old Wesleyan chapel of 1881, opposite an austere house of symmetrical lines and long barns. Here meet the A605 again, at the S bend.

Take care in crossing over to The Red Lion, and hence to Eaglethorpe, a pleasing hamlet set back from the flurry of the road.

Follow the Nene Way signs down the lane to the small handgate, and notice the ancient dovecote, before the path meanders through a paddock to come out at the mill. Now deserted, it was first recorded as a working mill in the Domesday Book. On this site once stood Peterborough Abbey, Burystead Manor and the chapel of St Andrew.

The glorious high lantern tower at Fotheringhay beckons over the skyline, and there is a sight of Tansor, almost hidden by the trees, to the left. Be sure to visit the site of Fotheringhay Castle, to see the meagre fragments of the birthplace of Richard III, and the site of the imprisonment of Mary Queen of Scots.

On reaching Main Street in Fotheringhay, Garden Farm has

many historic connections, and you may pause to wonder at the superb church of St Mary and All Saints. Nearby is a lovely old house with a mansard roof, close to The Falcon, The Olde Forge (open to the public) and Blacksmith's Cottage. At the last house, turn right into the lane to Walcot Lodge Farm. Here the Nene Way proceeds to Nassington, and the circular walk commences. If you are continuing on the Nene Way, turn to Walk Sixteen.

The Walk: The walk begins at the opposite end of the village to the castle site. Follow the Nene Way through the Main Street and at the last house, where the Way goes right, turn left onto the lane.

At a pair of fingerposts on opposite sides, go through the scanty gap, right, in the high hedge, and staying next to the boundary, over two stiles.

On meeting the farm lane follow the signs, passing a mixed plantation, to a little spinney, where a waymark points through the young trees and over to a wooden slatted bridge. Make for the Anglian Water compound and on to the barns with protruding clay pipes and steep pitched roofs, to the Oundle Road, facing Meadow View. Turn right here to the road junction and painted Woodnewton village sign, not turning.

The notice board bears a plaque 'to celebrate 900 years of Norman Heritage', beside a convenient seat and phone box. Next comes the Old Saddlery, the corn merchant, and the welcoming White Swan hostelry. In the former Wesleyan chapel of 1840, a group of craftsmen, including a puppetmaker, wood carver, stencil-maker and potter, have created a workshop, which is well worth a ring at their bell to pause and drop in.

Before leaving Main Street, see the rather grand stone house, with the lofty chimney directly over the front door! Soon after comes the modern gateway and overhead lantern over the steps leading to St Mary's church, on the mound.

Turn into the lane, left, where two knobbly ash trees of great age grow on the verge in this precious corner of rural England. Conegar Farm stands in grandiose style over smooth lawns in this perfect setting, where the walker may briefly share the peaceful scene from the bridge over the brook.

Straight ahead now and up the gentle slope over the brow of the hill, where the vista is composed of outlying farms and vast but fragmented woodlands, spreading about the undulating wide-open spaces.

In the hollow, go over the bridge and on again, keeping to the rising riding and looking out for deer. Through the changing species of trees and wayside bracken, come down on the edge of the woods. Stay on the path as it sweeps around the corner, before leaving it at a broken-down stile and walking down the incline toward the village of Southwick and a quick glimpse of the Hall.

The leafy lane emerges next to the stark form of St Mary's church, and two posts signing to Kings Cliffe and to Apethorpe. Stay left for a lovely view of Southwick Hall (pub to the right), in spacious grounds, and for a little essential road walking.

After the double bend, where fingerpost points over the road, the path continues to the left, through the middle of the field, running parallel with (but not next to) the brook, and goes directly over the track from Southwick Grange, keeping the same line over the next three fields. At the fourth, it slants sharply right to a small bridge and keeps a similar angle over the next two fields to finish opposite Perio Mill, a name derived from 'a spur of land marked by a pear tree'.

Historical Notes

Warmington (Nene Way): The majority of the old buildings are of stone quarried at Barnack, which was used in the broach spire of the church of St Mary the Virgin. There is a wealth of decoration on the west door and in the rich interior of this building.

Eaglethorpe (Nene Way): The 17th century limestone dove-cote, now scheduled an Ancient Monument, contains almost 800 nesting boxes.

Fotheringhay: Much has been written about the history of the castle and, standing on the mound, one can almost taste the flavour of those turbulent times.

Listed in the Domesday Book as 'Fodringea', the name indicates 'enclosure', which was an apt description of the location when Rockingham Forest swathed the landscape. Travellers, at risk of life and limb when robbers and murderers roamed the dark woods, must have been relieved at the sight of such lantern towers, which guided them to shelter.

The early motte and bailey on this spot was built around 1100 for Simon de Senlis, Earl of Northampton and Hunting-don. He took as his bride Maude, daughter of Judith, niece of the Conqueror and a prominent landowner.

The castle was rebuilt in the 14th century by Edmund de Langley, fifth son of Edward II and founder of the House of York. He started to build a college, attached to the church, and after his death it was founded by his son Edward, in 1411. He was to fall at Agincourt in 1415. John Dudley, Duke of Northumberland, demolished the seat of learning, gifted to him by Edward VI, following the Dissolution. This left the truncated church of today.

Elizabeth I when visiting Fotheringhay, ordered new monu-ments to her Plantagenet ancestors, Edmund, Duke of York, and his son Richard, the third Duke, who had perished at Wakefield. She was also responsible for the rebuilding of the bridge, further downstream than the present crossing, at a cost of £180 in 1573.

Mary Queen of Scots languished in the castle as a prisoner

from 1586, through her trial and execution in the Great Hall in February 1587, when she was beheaded. She had been held in captivity for 18 years and died with dignity at the age of 44, when her death warrant had been reluctantly signed by her cousin Elizabeth. Her heart was buried in the grounds of the castle and her body wrapped in a cloth and laid in a lead coffin, remaining unburied for six months, before being conveyed to Peterborough Cathedral. It was ultimately removed to Westminster Abbey, in 1612, to lie with the ranks of royal personages.

Demolished in 1628, the stone from the fated castle was redistributed for rebuilding at Fineshade, Oundle and various places around the county.

Garden Farm, built by Edward IV as the New Inn, faces the street, with an interesting Gothic arch. Used to house the overflow, or perhaps less important guests, it is thought that the queen's executioner, Bull, was billeted here.

The dazzling church of St Mary and All Saints conjures up visions of the past and has played a major role in English history. Wonderful, bold flying buttresses range the outer walls and the octagonal lantern tower tops the battlements and pinnacles, which form a landmark for miles around. The noble proportions of the edifice, though less now than in its heyday, are quite spectacular. Though the long windows admit bright light, the atmosphere reeks of mystery. Elizabethan memorials and treasures await the visitor, and it is said that medieval music is sometimes heard in this massive interior.

Woodnewton: The cruciform church of St Mary has a rebuilt tower from the 16th century and signs of earlier work in the nave, where one of the responds (carrying one end of an arch) has a row of carved human heads.

Referred to as 'Newtone' in the Domesday Book, the village not long ago had a blacksmith, slaughterhouse and washhouse, where the water was drawn from underground by the local washerwoman.

The world famous character Coco the Clown, in reality Russian-born Nicolai Polakovs OBE, chose the village as his home between his travels with the circus. When he died, in 1974, he was buried in this churchyard.

The White Swan has had a chequered existence. It was closed down in 1988, at a great loss to the community. However, the pub was rescued from the final indignity by a public outcry, and now presents a charming venue in the midst of this appealing village.

Southwick: Southwick Hall, a family home dating from the 14th century, is a fine example of the country manor. It has been modified by succeeding owners, by the addition of new wings and stables, and stands in expansive grounds. It is open mainly on summer weekends.

St Mary's church tower and spire were built around 1350 by Sir John Knyvet, early owner of the neighbouring Hall and Lord Chancellor to Edward III. It bears his shields and coat of arms. The church is guardian of a large memorial 'The Storied Urn' by Roubillac, in grey and white marble. It commemorates George Lynn, who died in 1758, showing a medallion of the deceased and a lady with folds of drapery, leaning against a classical urn.

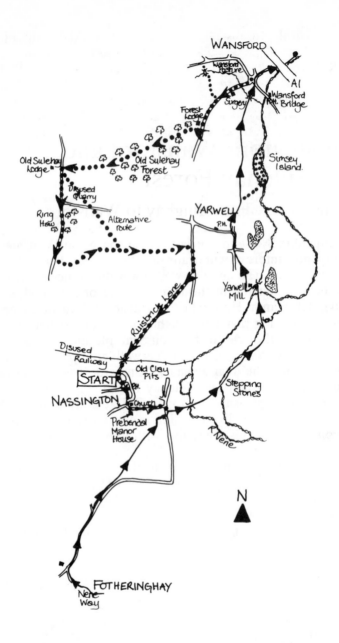

WANSFORD

Wansford Pasture

A1

Wansford Rd. Bridge

Surgery

Forest Lodge

Simsey Island.

Old Sulehay Lodge

Old Sulehay Forest

YARWELL

P.H.

Disused Quarry

Ring Haw

Alternative route

Yarwell Mill

Ruisbrick Lane

Disused Railway

Old Clay Pits

START

Stepping Stones

P.H.

NASSINGTON

Church

Prebendal Manor House

R. Nene

N

FOTHERINGHAY

Nene Way

Nassington, Wansford and Old Sulehay Forest

(Nene Way – Fotheringhay to Wansford)

Introduction: Now on the last lap of the Nene Way, neither beauty nor interest will wane as the walker heads for the county border. The circular walk joins the Nene Way on this last section, starting in the lovely village of Nassington. The Prebendal Manor House in the village is thought to be the earliest surviving residence in this county and dates from the 13th century, though it is built on Saxon foundations. Following the river Nene, through Yarwell and passing unusual Simsey Island, the Way reaches Wansford. The circular walk then returns through Old Sulehay Forest, once reserved 'for the Monarch's pleasure' and past Old Sulehay Lodge, where the King's Forester lived. Wildflowers, butterflies, birds and dragonflies bring this area alive with interest.

Distance: Fotheringhay to Wansford 5.3 miles. Circular walk roughly 7 miles. OS Landranger series 1:50 000 map 142 Peterborough.

Refreshments: The Black Horse, The Queen's Head and The Three Horseshoes are in Nassington. One public house in Yarwell, just off the route. Wansford has a number of establishments for refreshments, over the bridge in the main street.

How to get there: Nassington is halfway between Fotheringhay and Wansford, south of the A47 and north of the A605. The walk begins by All Saints church.

Nene Way – Fotheringhay to Wansford: This is the last stretch of the Nene Way. From Fotheringhay on the green lane, next to Park Spinney, follow the Nene Way signs over wide acres to the playing fields at Nassington, to exit on the Fotheringhay road. Now join the route of the circular walk, below, until the Way ends at Wansford.

The Walk: From All Saints church in Nassington, walk eastwards down the road towards the T junction. Turn right and join the Nene Way.

Across the road, next to the last house, with a fishing club notice on the field gate, go on to the stony track and over the quiet river bridge. Down the steps, a dozen elevated stepping-stones are set in a secluded bend of the stream (somewhat awkward for those with short legs!) where the water gurgles as it swishes around the curve.

Stay beside the brook and be alert for herons fishing on the isolated banks. Just skirt the poplar plantation, looking over the bridge for basking fish in summer sunshine and dragon-flies skimming the surface hunting their prey. A miniature stone footbridge is an interesting feature on the way to Yarwell Mill, and do not be alarmed to see parachutists descending, from nearby Sibson airfield!

Over the millrace, the widespread lakes provide a peaceful setting in this well kept caravan park. It is an idyllic backwater, with an old grinding wheel at the gate.

A few yards up the hill, the Nene Way sign on the steep verge directs you to Yarwell and along the main street. On the corner bend at Yarwell House, the walk goes between more mellowed walls festooned with thick trails of ivy.

After the first field out of Yarwell, a detour may be taken to the unique Simsey Island, over the sluice. It is privately owned, but the public are able to enjoy this unusual place. At the far end of the plot, The Dingle is a compact, wild section, bordered by a ditch, which at one time marked the former Huntingdon/Northamptonshire border.

Returning to the Nene Way, continue to Wansford, soon to see the ten arches of this famous old bridge (with ten corresponding cutwaters above). This section may be inclined to be squelchy all year round.

The mellowed buildings of this ancient settlement are a joy to behold and well worth a temporary departure from the circuit, over the bridge, particularly to the Haycock Inn and the miscellany of cafes and small shops for browsing.

Turn to the left and hug the wall of the parish church of St Mary, with its dumpy broach spire and sombre evergreen yews overhanging worn headstones, a familiar scene in our village churchyards. This bushy tree often has a number of vertical stems intertwined and forms a valuable habitat for wildlife. For centuries, man utilised this timber for making bows, which were essential for the dwellers of the forest.

The **Nene Way now** comes to an end. It departs along the Peterborough Road to the right, down a concrete ramp just prior to the A1, and goes under two arches of the bridge, differing vastly in design though with a single purpose, to the neighbouring county of Cambridgeshire where it ends.

To continue on the circular walk go left down the hill on the Yarwell Road and up again, past the deer warning. A post in the hedgerow shows the public footpath to Wansford Pasture, a Northants Wildlife Trust Reserve, and soon after, a dilapidated old loghouse stands crumbling in the spinney.

Carry on to where the view opens up to the distant A1, and the modern bustle of heavy traffic appears incongruous over the placid rooftops of Wansford.

Just after Forest Lodge, follow the post 'bridleway to Sulehay' through a handgate on the right. A protracted shady path through Old Sulehay Forest eventually ends at the 17th century Sulehay Lodge set back from the road.

(A path at this gateway doubles back to wind through the disused quarry for those who might wish to study the wild flora and fauna, and carries on to meet the suggested route.)

A little road walking now to the next corner, to the left, on the Yarwell Road, but go straight over the leafy byway, cutting through between Ring Haw and Whitelaw Coppice. In about ½ mile, a set back post pointing left reads 'to Yarwell', initially by the remains of a fallen wall. In the first field, keep to the right of the hedge and go through a gap in the second field. Go immediately diagonally right to another gap for a short way before crossing back (this joins the path from the quarry).

Straight on now to meet the road on the outskirts of Yarwell. Turn to the right for a little way, to Ruisbrick Lane. This leads into Nassington, under the disused railway line and by the site of the defunct clay pits.

Go over the ford and up into the village, bearing left at the triangle to Church Street. Here you will find The Three Horseshoes, the Prebendal Manor House and dovecote, All Saints' church, the Wesleyan chapel of 1872, Nassington House, the village hall and school, along with lovely houses and quaint barn conversions, lining the wide street.

Historical Notes

Yarwell: The name may mean 'a spring by which the yarrow grows'. Not far from Yarwell Mill, a pleasant lake area and old millstream, is the junction for the Nene Valley Railway, which operates between Wansford Station (at Stibbington), Yarwell and Ferry Meadows Country Park, to Peterborough.

Simsey Island, a lozenge-shaped islet is privately owned, but has a dedicated footpath. It has a lock to one side and a weir on the other, as well as the remains of a wharf. This is indicative of the former paper-mills, where two watermills and a fulling mill are noted in 1619 by a Stibbington man in his will. The ensuing production of paper, made from rags, serviced several news-papers including The Times, until an explosion in 1855 rocked the mill and wrecked the factory, and business finally ceased in 1859.

Wansford: Wansford, at the end of the Way, has its own inimitable tale in the story of a local man, Barnaby, in the time of George III. Barnaby fell asleep, in mid-summer, on a haycock in the riverside meadows. Oblivious to all, he was swept off in a storm downstream. When he awoke, partly under the arches of the bridge, he looked up to the villagers on the parapet and enquired his whereabouts. The answer floated down 'In Wansford'. He replied incredulously 'Wansford-in-England?', believing he had been carried far afield, or perhaps even out to sea. Ever since, the village has often been referred to by this name, and even the local hostelry The Haycock has a sign illustrating the story.

Clay, thought to have been dug from pits to the west of Wansford, was once brought here to Roman kilns, where pots were fashioned and possibly distributed by means of the river, a major trade route.

The Haycock Inn, at the end of the bridge, was a coaching inn from the 18th century, serving travellers converging from Oundle, Peterborough, Huntingdon, Stamford and Leicester, and consequently an important crossing.

Originally constructed from timber donated by Henry III in 1234, from the forest of Cliffe, the bridge was later replaced in the 16th and 17th centuries by stone from nearby quarries. It thus bears several date stones as additions and repairs were made, the last arch being added in 1795. This was a thriving river port, where barges unloaded their cargoes of coal and grain, and took away building stone and timber from the surrounding forest.

Old Sulehay Forest comprises the compartments of Wansford Quarter, Mortar Pits, Cow Wood and Kings Oak. Where 'hay' is incorporated in a forest name it usually indicates an enclosure within the woodland fenced off for hunting. In Cliffe Bailiwick, Old Sulehay was reserved exclusively for 'the Monarch's pleasure', whilst the villages of Yarwell and Nassington among others held common rights in the forest.

Old Sulehay Lodge, a gabled house with mullioned windows, set in the dense forest, was the residence of the King's Forester. A profusion of wildflowers carpet the floor of the woodland here in summer. Spotted flycatchers, warblers and chiff-chaff flit through the branches, and in winter the place is alive with yellow-streaked siskin and the swift sparrowhawk hunting for prey. The adjacent disused quarries provide a paradise for many species of dragonfly that hover over the limpid pools, and bright butterflies wing over the myriad flora on the limy soil.

Nassington: It is suggested that the Prebendal Manor House is the earliest surviving residence in this county. Dating from the 13th century, the stone manor is flanked by a 16th century dovecote and tithe barn.

The prebends (holding a stipend allotted from the revenue of a cathedral, in this case Lincoln) of Nassington occupying the manor were prominent men, such as Simon of Sudbury, who was both Archbishop of Canterbury and Lord Chancellor. He was killed in the Peasants' Revolt in 1381.

Underneath a part of the grounds, excavations revealed post holes relating to a royal manor, probably owned by King Canute in the 10th century. Examination of an old gravel pit near to the river, recovered a collection of grave items, including spearheads and jewellery, from an Anglo-Saxon cemetery.

The Manor House is open to the public on certain days, and is owned by English Heritage.